Maximum
Mentoring

**CORWIN
PRESS**

The Corwin Press logo—a raven striding across an open book—represents the happy union of courage and learning. We are a professional-level publisher of books and journals for K-12 educators, and we are committed to creating and providing resources that embody these qualities. Corwin's motto is "Success for All Learners."

Maximum Mentoring

An Action Guide for Teacher Trainers and Cooperating Teachers

Gwen L. Rudney   Andrea M. Guillaume

Foreword by Ellen Moir

CORWIN PRESS, INC.
A Sage Publications Company
Thousand Oaks, California

For information:

Corwin Press, Inc.
A Sage Publications Company
2455 Teller Road
Thousand Oaks, California 91320
www.corwinpress.com

Sage Publications Ltd.
6 Bonhill Street
London EC2A 4PU
United Kingdom

Sage Publications India Pvt. Ltd.
B-42 Panchsheel Enclaive
New Delhi 110 017 India

Printed in the United States of America

Library of Congress Cataloging-in-Publication Data

Library of Congress Cataloging-in-Publication Data
Rudney, Gwen L.
Maximum mentoring: An action guide for teacher trainers and cooperating teachers /
Gwen L. Rudney, Andrea M. Guillaume.
     p. cm.
Includes bibliographical references and index.
ISBN 0-7619-4635-7 (Cloth) -- ISBN 0-7619-4636-5 (Paper)
   1. Mentoring in education-Handbooks, manuals, etc.
2. Teachers-In-service training-Handbooks, manuals, etc. 3. First-year teachers-Training of-Handbooks, manuals, etc. I. Guillaume, Andrea M. II. Title.
LB1731.4 .R83 2003
370'71'5--dc21

                         2002153651

This book is printed on acid-free paper.

03 04 05 06 10 9 8 7 6 5 4 3 2 1

Acquisitions Editor:	Faye Zucker
Editorial Assistants:	Julia Parnell and Stacy Wagner
Production Editor:	Melanie Birdsall
Copy Editor:	Meredith L. Brittain
Typesetter:	C&M Digitals (P) Ltd.
Proofreader:	Nancy Lambert
Indexer:	Sheila Bodell
Cover Designer:	Tracy E. Miller
Production Artist:	Michelle Lee

Contents

Foreword

still remember my excitement and pride 30 years ago as I turned the key and walked through the door to my first classroom. The bare room smelled of varnish and chalkdust. As I began the task of turning this empty space into a learning community, I felt very alone. Throughout the entire first year, aside from an occasional observation from my principal, I navigated the complexities of teaching by myself. I made lots of mistakes. Sometimes I learned from these mistakes, and sometimes I had no idea what to do. I survived the first year, but I can only imagine how much better a teacher I would have been that year if I'd had a mentor.

Times have changed. We no longer use the trial-by-fire method to induct new teachers. In the same way that physicians learn to practice medicine through a residency program, student teachers and beginning teachers need the guidance of skilled mentors to become effective educators.

Maximum Mentoring provides a timely and important contribution to building effective teacher education and induction programs. Nearly two million new teachers will enter U.S. classrooms over the next decade. Since teacher quality is the single most important component of student success, nothing is more crucial for our schools than supporting our new teachers as they enter the profession. This book demonstrates how experienced, talented teachers—trained as mentors—can enhance preservice and induction programs.

Good teachers know how to teach; good mentors know how to help a novice learn to teach. It is critical that we look at what a cooperating teacher or mentor teacher needs to know to support a student teacher or new teacher. Mentors can help provide a supportive environment where beginning teachers can take risks and explore their new role as an educator. Talented mentors help student teachers and beginning teachers reflect on their teaching and set appropriate goals for professional learning. They also help novices assess their strengths and areas for growth as well as provide emotional support when the obstacles seem overwhelming.

Effective mentors have the ability to keep one eye on the new teacher's immediate needs and another eye on broader, professional concerns. Mentors know when to pose questions and when to provide concrete advice. They have good observational skills and know how to give useful feedback. Effective mentors have strong interpersonal communication skills as well as patience, generosity of spirit, and an inquiring disposition.

In the 20 years that I worked as a Supervisor of Teacher Education at the University of California, Santa Cruz, I have seen the key role that cooperating teachers play in helping student teachers succeed. Each year I strove to find the best placements for our students. I'd ask myself, is this cooperating teacher someone I'd enjoy learning from? I was always looking for excellent teachers with the disposition and qualities of an outstanding mentor.

In 1988, I developed the Santa Cruz New Teacher Project (SCNTP), a program to support newly credentialed teachers. I knew that providing new teachers with mentoring from outstanding veteran teachers would be the foundation of the program. After fifteen years work supporting nearly 8,000 beginning teachers, the SCNTP maintains this focus. We release experienced teachers fulltime to work with beginning teachers—in their classrooms—during the school day. And we have learned a lot about what it takes to help experienced teachers learn their new role as mentors.

Mentoring is sometimes misperceived as an intuitive and informal role. To be an effective mentor takes time and training. It requires a whole new set of skills. *Maximum Mentoring* offers an array of training strategies for mentors, and helps to codify what it means to be an effective mentor. Gwen Rudney and Andrea Guillaume clearly understand the complexities of the roles of cooperating teacher, mentor, and supervisor. They share a wide array of examples that employ adult learning theories, encourage relationship building with novices, use standards as a foundation for formative and summative assessment, and detail strategies for working with struggling novices. I'm particularly impressed with their deep understanding of the needs of novices and their applied ideas on how well-trained, knowledgeable cooperating teachers form the cornerstone of an effective teacher preparation and induction program.

An investment in teacher quality starts at the earliest stages of teachers' careers and continues throughout their professional lives. Using the talent of our nation's exemplary teachers to support novices benefits the entire profession. It offers veteran teachers a chance to share their wealth of knowledge while adding another professional dimension to teaching.

Maximum Mentoring makes great sense. It is a wonderful resource for mentors who want to contribute to the next generation of teachers.

Ellen Moir, Executive Director
The New Teacher Center
University of California, Santa Cruz

Acknowledgments

The authors and publisher would like to acknowledge the contributions of the following reviewers:

Judy D. Butler
Assistant Professor of Secondary Education
Department of Curriculum and Instruction
State University of West Georgia
Carrollton, GA

Kathleen Chamberlain
Assistant Professor of Education
Lycoming College
Williamsport, PA

Richard Frerichs
Department of Educational Foundations
Millersville University
Millersville, PA

Sylvia Roberts
Associate Professor
School of Education
City College of New York
New York, NY

Susan Tauer
Assistant Professor
Assumption College
Worcester, MA

About the Authors

 **Gwen L. Rudney**, Ph.D., is an Associate Professor of Education at the University of Minnesota, Morris. Her teaching and research interests include classroom processes, teacher development, multicultural education, and working with parents. She has worked with student teachers and cooperating teachers in regional, national, and international field placements. She may be reached via e-mail at rudneygl@mrs.umn.edu.

 **Andrea M. Guillaume**, Ph.D., is a Professor in the Department of Elementary and Bilingual Education at California State University, Fullerton. Her fields of interest include teacher cognition and development, and content area instruction. She works with practicing and prospective teachers through Professional Development Schools and through a teacher induction project. She may be reached via e-mail at aguillaume@fullerton.edu.

1

Introduction

First Things First

Thank you for picking up this book, and thank you for turning to Chapter 1. Those simple actions indicate your commitment to helping teachers new to our profession and provide an invitation for us to work together as you assume the vital role of mentor for the next generation of teachers. With the growing recognition that teachers at all points in their career path can benefit from the support of a knowledgeable and trusted professional, the roles of a mentor are now many. As a cooperating teacher (or master teacher), you provide leadership by guiding the apprenticeship, the classroom-based portion of student teachers' professional education. As a support provider (or mentor teacher), you provide collaborative opportunities for new teachers to explore and reflect on their practice in a safe setting, and you enhance the professional community of education through your efforts to build collegiality.

Cooperating teacher, yours is a memorable role. We know from working with hundreds of student teachers that yours is the face that many of them will see in their mind's eye years from now. Yours is the voice that will speak to them from over their shoulder when

> "The one who teaches is the giver of eyes."
>
> —Tamil proverb
> (quoted in Creative Quotations, 2002)

they tackle a classroom dilemma five or ten years hence. Yours is a powerful role. The work you do as a cooperating teacher fosters success for our future teachers, and your influence has the potential to flavor the learning of our future teachers' many, many students for years to come. When you are effective in your role, you help student teachers gain richer insights into the complexities of the classroom, assist them in connecting what they learn through various sources and understanding its implications for actual students, foster effective practices, and shape future professionals' view of what it means to be a teacher. For these reasons, we are delighted to embark on your adventure with you, and we look forward to being a part of your thoughts as you do the important work of guiding a student teacher.

Support provider, the work you do for new inservice teachers is critical to the profession. We know that many new teachers perceive a sense of isolation, a lack of frequent feedback on their teaching, and an absence of sustained support. Without caring support from a fellow professional, many teachers leave teaching after just a few years in the classroom. The trusting relationship you build, the effective feedback you furnish, and the informal support you provide can make the difference between teachers' leaving or staying, between mere classroom survival and rich professional satisfaction. Your work is important, and we appreciate the opportunity to join you in your efforts.

> "Who finds a faithful friend, finds a treasure."
>
> —Jewish proverb
> (quoted in Creative Quotations, 2002)

ROLES FOR THOSE WHO MENTOR

Though local definitions vary, we use the noun *mentor* broadly to refer to one who supports, either formally or informally, a teacher's professional development. Three points at which formal mentoring often takes place include preservice field experiences, where the mentor is deemed a cooperating teacher; early inservice years, where the mentor is often referred to as a support provider; and later years, when the mentee experiences temporary or sustained troubles in the classroom or requests assistance that is focused on a specific need. The act of mentoring, of helping and providing counsel, takes on different flavors depending on the mentee's distance along the career path.

Cooperating Teacher

Cooperating teachers serve as early mentors by guiding the field-based portion of preservice teachers' training as they work toward initial licensure. Cooperating teachers are expected to be effective role models, to give control of their classrooms (in varying degrees) to the student teachers, and to provide feedback to the student teachers. The cooperating teacher role is distinctive in that cooperating teachers are expected to display superior classroom expertise and use well-honed communication skills for working with adults.

The cooperating teacher–student teacher relationship is the most unbalanced of the mentoring relationships. The fact that cooperating teachers provide formal evaluations—throughout the student teaching experience and at its culmination—brings about a very real power differential. Cooperating teachers have the power, through their evaluative role, to keep preservice teachers out of the profession of education.

Another type of mentor works with a preservice teacher who holds a paid classroom position but is currently enrolled in a credential program. Such mentees are usually called *interns,* though the terminology for their mentors varies. Some programs deem them *intern buddies,* and their role tends to be more of a supportive one than an evaluative one.

Support Provider

Many states fund programs that match new teachers with experienced colleagues during the new teachers' early years in the classroom, deemed the induction years. Additionally, many experienced teachers take on the role of support provider informally. Though the support provider's role varies by local program, the flavor of the support provider–mentee's relationship is very different from that of cooperating teacher–student teacher. First, the support provider is rarely in a position to provide summative, high-stakes evaluations of the mentee. Even when support providers act as assessors, the results of their assessments are usually formative and confidential. This relationship tends to be, then, more of an equal one, where the mentee perceives the support provider to have more experience but to be facing conditions similar to those the mentee is facing as a paid classroom teacher.

Peer Coach or Mentor

Some states fund programs that place experienced teachers in the role of mentor teacher or peer coach. In some states, mentors are hired to address curriculum and teacher development in certain clearly specified topics such as technology or writing instruction. In some places, experienced teachers assist others who either request aid in certain aspects of classroom practice (e.g., management) or who are required by their districts to improve their classroom practice or face possible termination. The stakes of the potential outcome of relationships between peer coaches or mentors and their mentees clearly color their interactions and the nature of their relationship.

Which role—or roles—do you play? Although the general goal of assistance and support crosses each type of mentoring relationship, "help" can mean different things in these different contexts. Keeping an explicit awareness of the purpose of your relationship and a recognition of the potential power you wield in your role as mentor can help you build a relationship and employ strategies that suit the formal expectations of your work.

YOUR RIGHTS AND RESPONSIBILITIES AS A MENTOR

Ours seems to be a profession where, during any given day, we juggle myriad responsibilities. In addition to your role as mentor, you no doubt hold a number of other responsibilities. Namely, many mentors continue to be responsible for the learning of a set of students. You probably also work on a number of committees or perform other professional duties.

Table 1.1 Balancing the Rights and Responsibilities of the Mentor's Role

Rights	*Responsibilities*
1. You have the right to expect ethical and professional behavior from your mentee.	1. You have the responsibility to model ethical and professional behavior for your new teacher partner.
2. As a cooperating teacher, you have the right to maintain final say for the educational decisions of your students.	2. You have the responsibility to provide freedom for your student teacher to experiment and develop a personal style and strategies.
3. You have the right to receive support from other members of the student teacher's team (e.g., university supervisor, course instructors) or the new teacher's team (e.g., other induction program leaders, the site administrator).	3. You have the responsibility to act as part of the team, providing information and working alongside team members such as the university supervisor, team leadership members, and the site administrator.
4. As a cooperating teacher, you have the right to use your professional expertise in the ways you believe best meet your students' needs and the needs of your student teacher.	4. You have the responsibility to remain open and consider other viewpoints and methods for meeting students' needs and the needs of your student teacher. You have the responsibility of acting flexibly to provide appropriate support to your mentee.
5. You have the right to expect sound, though developing, instructional practices from your student teacher.	5. You have the responsibility to direct your student teacher's growth in ways deemed appropriate by the profession. You have the responsibility to help your mentee deepen his or her practice in ways that support students' learning and enhance your mentee's professional satisfaction.
6. You have the right to contribute to the student teacher's evaluation.	6. You have the responsibility to give feedback that is frequent, honest, and caring.

The role of mentor adds another layer to your many professional responsibilities. It also brings a set of rights. Table 1.1 presents some of the rights and responsibilities to be balanced.

WHAT THIS BOOK DOES

We begin with the recognition that the work you do is critical to teachers' professional development. We begin with the understanding that there is a knowledge base and a set of perspectives and skills associated with the work of mentorship. And we begin with the conviction that, no matter how experienced one is, one can and should grow in one's capacity to serve as an effective mentor. The purpose of this text is to provide support for *you* as you support future teachers' development.

As a support, this text strives to meet three goals. First, it attempts to provide some key information related to many facets of teacher development and the practice of mentoring. Second, it provides opportunities for you and your mentee to build a common ground and to maintain a successful working relationship. To accomplish these aims, each chapter offers some key ideas and practical advice and includes exercises that may be useful as you and your mentee build and sustain an effective professional relationship.

Our hope is that this text will provide guidance and direction as you manage the many roles and responsibilities of your important work as mentor. You are embarking on an important journey in the life of a new teacher. We look forward to traveling with you. Good wishes.

> "The beginning is always today."
>
> —Mary Shelley Wollstonecraft
> (quoted in Creative Quotations, 2002)

A Note on Language Use

In addition to the word "mentee," we use a number of terms to represent new teachers. Mentees are also called "new teacher partners" as a general term applying to all mentees, "preservice teachers" or "student teachers" as terms applying to interns and credential candidates, and "newly credentialed teachers" as those in their first years of teaching.

EXERCISES

Exercise 1.1 Recording Your Roles and Responsibilities

Explore the work that lies ahead through this checksheet.

Roles and Responsibilities	✓ When Answered	Notes
1. What are my formal responsibilities?		
2. What is my role as an evaluator (e.g., formative and summative)?		
3. What are the potential benefits and pitfalls of the partnership for me professionally and personally?		
4. What else do I need to know right now?		
(Other)		

Exercise 1.2   Setting a Purpose to Read

We know that strong readers and active learners have a purpose in mind as they approach a learning situation. Try taking some notes on what you want to learn in reading this book. Then skim ahead and jot down possible chapters or page numbers that may hold information that is relevant for your purposes. If you do not find what you need, let us know, or ask people in your local context.

What do I hope to learn from this book?	In which chapter or on which page might it be found? Where might I find more information?

Exercise 1.3   Let's Go Surfing Now

Though it has its drawbacks, the Internet is a powerful tool for gaining and sharing information about mentoring. Sites change so frequently that we do not list individual Web addresses. Instead, we recommend a variety of meta search engines and search terms to set you on your way. Happy surfing!

Helpful Meta Search Engines	*Promising Search Terms*

www.google.com
 	
    Comprehensive. Try "advanced search" for more specificity.
 	
www.ixquick.com
 	
    Powerful.
 	
http://vivisimo.com
 	
    Sorts results in a tree structure so you can travel quickly to the appropriate category.
 	
www.zworks.com
 	
    Uses Boolean logic, so you can be very specific in your search terms.
	Use the following phrases:
	
	    mentor teacher
	    teacher induction
	    new teachers
	    cooperating teachers
	    teacher education

Also try:

- Going to your state's Department of Education Web site and looking for mentoring projects.
- Going to the Educational Resources Information Center (ERIC) Clearinghouse for Teaching and Teacher Education (www.ericsp.org).

2

Teacher Development

In this chapter, we trace the *predictable* development of preservice and beginning teachers' reasoning, concerns, and abilities throughout the teacher preparation program and first year or so of teaching. Of course, you know that no one will perfectly match the predictable pattern and that there will always be individual variation. Still, we think that alerting you to frequent developmental patterns will provide you with a context in which to understand your partner. Examination of preservice and beginning teachers' perceptions and concerns can lead to insight about the problems teachers face and the knowledge they value.

You have considerable expertise in teacher development—having lived it and watched it in others—but it may be *unexamined* expertise. You may not have thought about how your experience exemplifies or differs from general experiences. Before reading, think about your own individual story of development. Even if it was a LONG time ago, try to remember! Here are some questions to consider:

- What worries and activities occupied most of your time and thoughts during your student teaching experience? At the end, what was your main growth area?
- As a new teacher, what main tasks did you work to accomplish? What were your most consistent concerns?
- How are you *different* now than you were as a first-year teacher? What has experience taught you?

In the next section, you can compare your answers to what we know from the study of teacher development. We present three major research studies often used as reference points in the discussion of preservice and inservice teacher growth. We also share the results of our own research and experience in working with student teachers. In each of the studies, analysis of data leads to notions of how best to understand and explain the complex and amazing process of learning to teach. None of the studies is perfect. All can be useful. What do you find most compelling?

THE CONCERNS AND REFLECTIONS OF STUDENT TEACHERS

"When we have nothing to worry about we are not doing much, and not doing much may supply us with plenty of future worries."

—Chinese proverb
(quoted in Creative Quotations, 2002)

The work of Fuller (1969) and Fuller and Bown (1975) has influenced the way we think about beginning teachers. Based on the analysis of empirical research, Fuller and Bown suggested that student teachers move through four stages of concern. In the first stage, prior to any teaching, preservice (or pre-preservice), teachers are concerned with themselves as pupils. They realistically perceive what student life is like but have unrealistic or "fantasy" images of teachers. As one of our preservice teachers reported after his first classroom experience, "I was completely overwhelmed. I had no idea of all that was involved in teaching." His comment also introduces the second stage—concern with survival. In this stage, the budding teachers worry about their ability to fulfill basic obligations of the teaching role. In the next stage, student teachers have teacher or task concerns, and they focus particularly on the demands of their current experience. Finally, in the last stage, they evidence student impact concern— that is, they begin to focus on the skills of teaching and the needs of students. Though some research studies have supported the proposed stages of development, others—including our own (Guillaume & Rudney, 1993)—have revealed limitations to the findings. The "stages" are neither distinct nor consistently ordered (Burden, 1990).

Programmatic and individual differences may explain conflicting results. Though teacher education programs adhere to similar goals, there are multiple variations in meeting the objectives. For instance, programs may vary in length, and the amount, setting, and sequence of field experiences may differ. It will be important for you to ask your student teacher and the university supervisor about the kind of program offered. A newly credentialed teacher partner's current thinking may similarly be related to the preservice program he or she experienced. Of course, personal factors also explain differences in development. Some concerns may relate to gender (Pigge & Marso, 1987) or cognitive structures (Winitzky, 1990). Many believe that students enter teacher education programs with stable—and resistant—belief systems that are based in part on their own experiences in elementary and secondary school (Zeichner & Liston, 1987).

NOVICE TEACHERS AND HOW THEY DIFFER FROM YOU

David Berliner (1988) drew from a general theory of expertise, applied it specifically to teaching, and developed another way to view teacher development. In his analysis of the cognitions underlying novice and expert performances in teaching, he described five stages through which a teacher *may* move throughout a career. The five stages, displayed in Table 2.1, are Novice, Advanced Beginner, Competent, Proficient, and Expert.

Novices label and learn elements of classroom tasks. Their teaching is relatively inflexible and requires purposeful concentration. Novices and advanced beginners may not understand what it is important to notice. They are also learning what is supposed to happen and, unlike an expert, may not yet be able to distinguish the typical from the atypical. Experts, on the other hand, tend to make predictions confidently, have well-established routines, and expect things to go well.

In general, Berliner focuses on the role of experience in moving toward competence and higher stages of teaching. He relates it to the role experience plays in the development of more comprehensive schemata—that is to say fuller, more complex, and internalized understandings of the classroom. Sources of expertise are adequate planning time, knowledge of students, personal history, reputation, and routinized performance. Not all teachers will reach the proficient stage, and only a very small number will become experts. Berliner suggests that expertise is actually quite fragile because it is highly contextualized and may not transfer well. So, in fact, depending on the circumstances or setting, an expert may not *always* be an expert.

According to this research, novice teachers need emotional support, assistance focused on the learning of classroom routines and processes, and experience. In working with your novice or beginning teachers, you will be a key provider of what they need. Let them know that you have faith in their abilities to work with students and to continue their own growth as professionals. Help them understand the importance of planning, and give them feedback on their performance. In addition to supporting their creativity, provide the inexperienced beginners with materials, plans, and manuals that will help them get started. To gain competence, beginners need experience that includes decision-making power and responsibility. Cooperating teachers can structure student teaching activities that allow student teachers the freedom to make decisions. As they gain experience, you can help them understand the importance of planning and support their implementation and assessment of lessons. New teachers will benefit from mentor support as they shoulder the decision-making responsibilities of their own classrooms.

What if I am not an expert? That is a good question. We say, don't worry about it. We suggest that you reflect on your own interpretation of classroom events and think about where you would place yourself on the chart, but we are not sure how one reliably and validly determines where someone fits into the specific stages. You are certainly competent and, if you are like most professionals, you have specific areas of special knowledge and skill. You probably have flashes of brilliance! Berliner himself states that a competent teacher "may be able to articulate as well or better than the expert the issues of pedagogy that must be addressed by the novice and advanced beginner" (Berliner, 1988, p. 61). Though "experts" can provide excellent modeling for the new professional, a key element of successful mentorship is the ability to explain and articulate the act of teaching.

If you examine the stages of expertise in Table 2.1, you will see that the stages progress from deliberate thought about action and decision making toward

Table 2.1   Expertise in Teaching

Stage	Teachers Included	Tasks and Processes
1. Novice	Many student teachers and first-year teachers, often from alternative licensure paths	<ul><li>Label and learn essential tasks</li><li>Label and describe events</li><li>Acquire and follow "context-free" rules (such as wait 3 seconds after asking a high-order question)</li><li>Learn the objective facts and features</li><li>Gain experience</li><li>Rely on deliberative thought process</li></ul>
2. Advanced Beginner	Some first-year teachers and many in their second or third year	<ul><li>Meld experience and verbal knowledge</li><li>Recognize similarities across contexts</li><li>Use context to guide behavior</li><li>Rely on deliberative thought process</li></ul>
3. Competent	Many third- and fourth-year teachers as well as more experienced teachers	<ul><li>Make conscious choices about what they do by setting priorities and making plans</li><li>Know what is important—what to attend to and what to ignore</li><li>Feel responsible for and connected to classroom events</li><li>Rely on deliberative thought process</li></ul>
4. Proficient	At about their fifth year of teaching, some teachers will enter this stage	<ul><li>Understand and adapt to situations accurately but unconsciously</li><li>Predict events more precisely</li><li>Understand classroom typicality holistically</li><li>Rely on intuition-based experience</li></ul>
5. Expert	A select number of experienced teachers	<ul><li>Intuitively grasp situations</li><li>Perform fluidly with seemingly little analysis or deliberation</li><li>Go with the flow</li><li>Process *unexpected* events analytically and deliberately</li></ul>

SOURCE: Drawn from the work of Berliner (1988) and Cushing, Sabers, and Berliner (1992)

seemingly unconscious, automatic performance. If you are in the intuitive stage, the act of teaching may feel natural, like common sense. Remember that for the student or beginning teacher, it is not effortless. Your partner is learning a complex task, and you can help him or her interpret the skills, rules, and subtleties of the undertaking.

THE TASKS NOVICE TEACHERS ACCOMPLISH

From an analysis of dozens of studies that examined the experiences of practice and beginning teachers, Kagan (1992) inferred three fundamental tasks that novice teachers must accomplish during their teacher preparation and first year of teaching. Novice teachers acquire knowledge of pupils, use the knowledge to modify and reconstruct their image of themselves as teachers, and develop procedural routines that integrate classroom management and instruction.

Knowledge of Pupils

Novice teachers have perceptions of pupils based largely on their image of themselves as pupils. For that reason, they are often surprised that young students do not behave in a way that they expected. Extensive and structured experience in classrooms is vital to increased knowledge of pupils. Assignments that require student teachers to step back and examine beliefs and actions are useful in supporting their growth.

Image of Self as Teacher

Growing knowledge of and structured experiences with pupils, along with a careful *inward* reflective focus, will assist novice teachers in reshaping their images of self as teacher. Novices firmly hold to images and beliefs—based on their personal histories, experiences, and personalities—that may not match reality and are likely insufficient for effective teaching. The cognitive dissonance experienced by novices when working with pupils, cooperating teachers, mentors, and others who hold or exemplify conflicting views will result in a changing image.

Integrated Procedural Routines

The need to understand and implement effective routines for instruction and management is paramount for novices. An idealized view of pupils and an oversimplified vision of classroom practice may result in a novice teacher's inability to manage a classroom. He or she may plan instructional activities based not on student learning needs but rather on student discipline needs. With support, novices can learn procedures that work in the classroom and thus be free to focus on the actions and activities that result in student learning.

> "The beginnings and endings of all human undertakings are untidy."
>
> —John Galsworthy (quoted in Creative Quotations, 2002)

According to Kagan (1992), three factors influence novices' learning of the developmental tasks. First, their growth is affected by their own biography—their images, experiences, and readiness to face their own problematic perspectives. Next, the context of their teacher preparation program is influential. What courses are required? How are field experiences implemented? What assignments are given? Finally, the specific context for student teaching or the first year of teaching will affect how the novice matures into a competent teacher. Particularly significant to the context is the administrator's comfort with teacher autonomy and the relationship the novice develops with you, the experienced teacher partner.

CATEGORIES OF CONCERN AND CHANGES THAT OCCUR

We see that preservice teachers can be reflective and move from thinking about educational matters in concrete, undifferentiated ways to thinking in ways that are more integrated, flexible, and holistic (Guillaume & Rudney, 1993). From our work with student teachers, we have found that they evidence a broad range of concerns that they address seriously *throughout* their student teaching. The concerns fall into six major categories:

- Lesson Planning and Evaluation
- Discipline
- Working With Pupils
- Working With Cooperating Teachers and Adjusting to Their Classrooms
- Working With Others in the Profession
- Transition From Student to Professional Teacher

In contrast to Fuller and Bown (1975), who found that student teachers had different concerns over time, we found that as they progress through preparation programs, student teachers do not so much think about *different things* as they grow; rather, they think about *things differently*. Table 2.2 presents the changes student teachers show in the categories of concern and thus paints a picture of their development from early, to mid, and then to advanced student teachers. Teacher educators—including cooperating teachers and mentors—can support this process. By recognizing that student teachers are inquiring in order to move toward independence in their teaching, and by supporting inquiry through reflective teaching that encourages them to question and analyze their practice and experiences, we can help in the development of thoughtful teachers struggling to construct more complex ways of thinking and more independent patterns of action. Box 2.1 provides suggested questions and activities to help you understand and support your mentee's growth toward independence.

Table 2.2   Student Teachers' Changing Concerns

Concern	Early Field Experience	Mid-Program	Late Student Teaching
Lesson Planning and Evaluation	• Extensive focus on individual lessons • Brief evaluations • Evaluations based on control and pupil attitude • Evaluations focus on what went well	• Lessons integrated within the day and week • More focus on evaluation rather than description • Evaluations focus on pacing and learning	• Broader scope: Long-term planning • Continued focus on elements other than control and pupil response • Evaluations focus on troublesome lesson segments
Discipline	• Acute concern • Identification with pupils • Questions about self as authority	• Acute concern • Applying particular strategies	• Acute concern • Search for the "key" to affecting pupils' behavior through legitimate authority
Working With Pupils	• Acute concern: Derive satisfaction from working with pupils • Struck by pupil diversity (ability, functioning, age)	• Acute concern: Derive satisfaction from working with pupils	• Acute concern: Derive satisfaction from working with pupils • Less emphasis on pupil diversity, more able to "chunk" information about pupils • Comments about pupils needing special help
Working With Cooperating Teachers and Adjusting to Their Classrooms	• Stable, acute concern • Interpret relationship in terms of own needs	• Stable, acute concern	• Stable, acute concern • More concerned about adjusting to the classroom rather than the classroom adjusting to them • Negotiated partnerships • Some relationships are strained

(Continued)

Table 2.2 Continued

Concern	Early Field Experience	Mid-Program	Late Student Teaching
Working With Others in the Profession	• Consistent, low concern • Concerned with parent involvement	• Consistent, low concern	• Consistent, low concern • Fewer comments about parents • More negative concerns about others
Transition From Student to Professional Teacher	• Trying on the role of "teacher" (sudden and enjoyable)	• Gradual progress and setbacks	• Transition dependent upon individual context, upon relationships with pupils and teacher, control and instruction

SOURCE: Drawn from the work of Guillaume and Rudney (1993)

A WORD ABOUT WORKING WITH ADULTS

"You cannot teach a man anything; you can only help him find it within himself."

—Galileo (quoted in Creative Quotations, 2002)

We hope we presented a compelling argument that your mentee can be expected to exhibit both a highly individualistic set of strengths, concerns, and approaches as well as a developmental trajectory that has been documented in the research. Your new teacher partner is developing in another sense as well. You can expect him or her, as an adult learner, to exhibit a number of goals and ways of looking at the world that are different from those of children. Adult learning theory (Brookfield, 1986; Knowles, 1980, 1984) specifies some principles that, when incorporated by experienced teacher partners, can support novices' struggles to master the art and science of teaching. In particular, adult learners are appear more self directed and goal oriented. Their extensive life experience influences the connections they make, the interactions they expect, and the opinions they readily form. You will discover their need for respect, relevance, and active learning.

THINKING ABOUT YOUR NEW TEACHER PARTNER'S THINKING

At the beginning of the chapter, we asked you to think about the worries and activities that occupied your time and thoughts during your preservice and beginning teaching experiences. How did your story follow the patterns of development

Box 2.1   Ways You Can Help

Guide Planning and Evaluation
- Ask to see plans in advance of teaching. What is the purpose for the lesson? What are the strengths of the plan?
- Check for sufficient management plans. Are procedures for handling supplies and movement present and adequate? Will your pupils understand the procedures?
- Help student teacher move to longer-term planning. How does the lesson align with previous and future lessons?
- Expect a variety of instructional strategies. Are different strategies included? Which seem easiest for your student teacher to implement? How can you assist him or her in successfully trying alternate strategies?
- Relate the planning and evaluation to student learning. Do assessment activities align with objectives? Does the student teacher assess student learning?

Guiding Discipline and Management
- Explain the discipline procedures that you have found most successful.
- Allow your student teacher to establish authority in ways that may be different from your own.
- Help your student teacher plan for management in your classroom, and debrief management issues after lesson implementation.
- Give both specific hints for classroom procedures and the rationale for their use.
- Think about and explain your classroom procedures. Where and when can pupils sharpen pencils? What is your policy for tardiness? How do you correct homework?
- Let your student teacher "hear you think." This will help in his or her own metacognition.
- During your observations, collect evidence related to your student teacher's management and discipline and help him or her draw conclusions from the evidence as you debrief. (For instance, you can record the amount of time spent during transitions or transcribe student teacher responses to student outbursts.)

Guiding Relationship With Pupils
- Help student teachers think about their image of themselves as pupil and their perception of the teacher actions and attitudes that helped them learn.
- Help them analyze how pupils will *differ* from their self-image and from each other.
- Help your student teacher analyze student performance data to look for clumps and trends and to discuss instructional implications.
- Keep pupil need and interests at the center of discussions concerning planning, instruction, and management.

- Provide opportunities for the student teacher to build a personal and professional relationship with the pupils in your classroom.
- Smile when the student teacher mentions that he or she is building a special relationship with a hard-to-reach student. The student teacher needs to feel needed, and a special relationship may indeed be developing.

Guiding Their Relationship With You and Others
- Remember your own experience.
- Treat student teachers as professionals.
- Provide faith, freedom, and feedback.
- Read Chapter 5 for suggestions on learning the classroom and school context.

described in the chapter? In what ways were your experiences different from the descriptions? It is likely that you can find examples in your experience that answer both of these questions. The same will be true for your student teacher or mentee. As a beginner, he or she will be immersed in experiences similar to those of other beginners, and he or she will share commonalties. As an individual, your partner will also bring unique experiences, talents, dispositions, and perspectives that will set him or her apart. Chapter 3 introduces you to a variety of ideas and activities that will help you to build a firm base for your relationship with your new teacher partner as an individual and as a professional. We hope that your relationship is enhanced by your knowledge of how new teachers grow and change as they join us in our profession.

EXERCISES

Exercise 2.1 Self-Study

At the beginning of the chapter, you answered several questions about your own experiences as a preservice and beginning teacher. Complete this chart as you reflect on your current stage of development and the things that brought you to this point.

When it comes to:	*I am often:*	*And here's when and why I think so:*
Understanding how students develop and learn	Competent Proficient Expert	
Meeting the needs of diverse learners in my classroom	Competent Proficient Expert	
Using my knowledge of subject matter to create appropriate lessons	Competent Proficient Expert	
Planning and implementing a variety of lesson strategies	Competent Proficient Expert	
Using authentic assessment to improve future learning	Competent Proficient Expert	
Communicating effectively with others in the profession	Competent Proficient Expert	
Collaborating with parents to improve student learning and my own practice	Competent Proficient Expert	
Other:	Competent Proficient Expert	

Exercise 2.2   Making Connections

Analyze the actions and comments of your preservice or beginning teacher partner and think about him or her in terms of one (or more) of the ways to view teacher development described in the chapter. Then answer the questions about development in general and your student in particular. Though this reflection is not a scientific analysis, others have found it useful.

Fuller & Bown: Concerns	Berliner: Stages of Expertise	Kagan: Tasks of Novices	Guillaume & Rudney: Changes in Thinking
○ Identification with pupils ○ Survival concerns ○ Task concerns ○ Student impact concerns	○ Novice ○ Advanced Beginner ○ Competent ○ Proficient ○ Expert	○ Knowledge of pupil ○ Knowledge of self as teacher ○ Integrated procedural routines	○ Early ○ Mid ○ Advanced

1. What evidence seemed most influential as you made your decisions? Did multiple sources of evidence support the same conclusion?

2. How well does your mentee "fit" in the schemes presented? Which behaviors seem typical for his or her current stage? Which behaviors seem atypical?

3. In what ways does your understanding of your mentee's likely concerns, skills, or ways of thinking help you to support your mentee's growth?

4. What are the limitations of stage theory for teacher development?

5. Do you want more practice? Read Exercise 7.1 in Chapter 7, the teaching case "Joe's First Lesson Observation." Analyze Joe's performance and worries to see if he is in a "typical" stage for a beginner.

6. Do you want more information? Try reading some of the research listed in the references for more detailed information.

Exercise 2.3 Study in Pictures

This exercise is a mini version of an experiment conducted at the University of Arizona and Arizona State University. Researchers there examined how beginning teachers and expert teachers view the classroom differently. After trying the exercise, read a summary of the actual study, which follows.

1. Become aware of how experienced teachers and novice or beginning teachers may have different—but reasonable—interpretations of classroom events.
   a. Examine—independently—the sequence of six pictures found after Step 3 of this exercise. Focus on anything you believe to be important for classroom management and instruction. Take as much time as you'd like.
   b. Record what you thought about.
   c. Share and compare your findings with your student teacher. How were they similar? What might explain any differences you found?

2. How did your responses compare to the study described after this exercise?
   a. Did the study's findings make sense to you? Why or why not?
   b. How can you personally balance your understanding of the level of development your student teacher has reached with your responsibility to help him or her grow in expertise?

3. Use this same technique to discuss an actual classroom event. How do your interpretations vary?

A

B

C

D

E

F

Olympic Gold: Investigations of Expertise in Teaching

Katherine S. Cushing, Donna S. Sabers, and David C. Berliner (1992) conducted a series of studies at the University of Arizona and Arizona State University that assessed how expert and novice teachers processed and perceived classroom information and events differently. They sought to add to the knowledge base about pedagogical expertise by asking the following questions:

- What is it that makes an expert teacher an expert?
- How do expert teachers resemble experts in other fields?

Participants in the study completed three processing tasks. The first was a simulation in which they were asked to plan and explain the first two days of instruction for a class that they were "taking over" six weeks into the school year. They were given classroom materials and student information. In the second task (the one similar to the exercise you just completed), the participants viewed and commented on 50 slides depicting a classroom lesson. The third task required the participants to simultaneously view three video monitors of classroom instruction and answer questions about what they saw.

Participants were selected from three levels of expertise. *Expert teachers* were experienced teachers—in this case, at the junior-high or senior-high level—who had been identified as outstanding by their supervisors. *Advanced beginners* were preservice teachers who had completed their student teaching or who were first year teachers. They had been identified as having the potential to develop into excellent teachers. *Novices* had no formal teacher training or experience in public school teaching but had expressed an interest in classroom teaching. Employed in business or industry, these individuals represented people who might use their expertise in other fields (e.g., computer technology) to pursue an alternate certification route.

What They Learned

Interesting contrasts among groups were found in each task, and three findings appeared consistent across tasks:

1. **Experts, advanced beginners, and novices differed in their perceptions and understanding of classroom events.** The authors described an interpretative-descriptive distinction in the responses. Experts tended to view visual material differently than either advanced beginners or novices. They either made hypotheses to explain or interpret the information present OR they cautiously refrained from interpreting the limited information presented to them. Beginners and novices typically provided literal and often valid descriptions of what they saw rather than interpreting the information.

2. **Experts, advanced beginners, and novices differed in the role they assumed in classroom instruction.** The experts tended to describe a more active, instructional role for the teacher. They were comfortable in assessing events and prescribing courses of action geared toward improvement. The novices and beginners tended once again to describe instruction or management concerns.

3. **Experts, advanced beginners, and novices differed in their notion of "typicality" within the classroom environment.** Experts have well-developed schemata for what is *typical* in classrooms. They tend to focus on what is *atypical* until they can make sense of it. Familiar with classroom *typicality,* experts also were better able to manage multiple tasks.

Reflection

How is this information helpful to teacher educators? Why are there few differences between novices and advanced beginners? In what ways might the experts' ability to make quick inferences interfere with their ability to collect data during an observation of their partners' teaching?

3

Building a Base for the Partnership

"A good cooperating teacher is a hero in the eyes of her student teacher."

—A student teacher

The quality of the relationship between the cooperating teacher and the student teacher is a critical factor in the novice's satisfaction and often success. Like the student teacher whose words are above, student teachers care very much about their relationship with their cooperating teacher (see, e.g. Sudzina & Coolican, 1994). Mounting evidence suggests that the same is true for newly credentialed teachers who are effectively mentored. Given the critical importance of the mentoring relationship, this chapter addresses two facets of building a base for the teacher partnership: building relationships through trust and understanding, and building effective communication strategies.

BUILDING RELATIONSHIPS THROUGH TRUST AND UNDERSTANDING

A key principle of adult learning is that facilitators should nurture learners' needs to become self-directed, proactive, and autonomous individuals (Brookfield, 1986) who have empathy for others' perspectives, monitor their own behavior, and assume responsibility for their actions. When people feel that they are perceived as trustworthy and capable of success, they are often freed to explore a broad range of practices, to make mistakes, and to analyze their own work in ways that encourage growth.

You Gotta Have Faith

Novices want very much for their mentors to trust in their ability to succeed, as these new teachers tell us:

- "My cooperating teacher told me that she had great faith in me as a teacher for her students."
- "My cooperating teacher treated me like a colleague."
- "She welcomed me as a peer."
- "She is kind and understanding even when I knew the lesson could have gone better."

Helping relationships are based on a firm foundation of acceptance and empathy (Rowley, 1999).

Our research with student teachers (Guillaume & Rudney, 2002) illustrates that they are indeed often intensely desirous that their cooperating teachers display faith in them, both as people and as budding professionals with a high probability of success. When asked about helpful strategies their cooperating teachers employed, many of our student teachers told us that they highly valued their cooperating teachers' efforts to build trusting, collegial relationships. The sidebar gives a few examples of student teachers' quotes related to trust and faith. Cooperating teachers who built effective relationships with their student teacher partners established a sense of acceptance, a spirit of collegiality, and an air of optimism about the student teacher's capacity for success. Lasley (1996) underscores the importance of faith by asserting that the crucial characteristics of a good mentor are conviction that a partner is capable of great accomplishments and willingness to share that conviction with the new teacher partner and others.

Trusting relationships are often built on shared experiences and perspectives, genuine affection, truthfulness, and development of a relationship over time as opportunities for trust are borne out and the partners continue to evidence trustworthiness. You'll find detailed and specific strategies for building trust during the first days of the partnership in Chapter 5. Some general approaches for establishing empathetic, trusting relationships include the following:

- Getting to know each other as people and as professionals
- Discussing and drawing from your partner's strengths and prior experiences
- Making the student teacher a presence in your classroom

"Those who trust us educate us."

—George Eliot
(quoted in Creative Quotations, 2002)

- Helping the new teacher understand the culture of schooling and of the school site
- Publicly supporting the authority of your partner
- Establishing a collegial rather than hierarchical relationship
- Demonstrating that you are also a learner who makes mistakes, reflects on practice, and will grow from your work with your partner
- Discussing the expectations you hold for each other and negotiating, to the extent possible, common ground

Getting to Know Each Other as People

Part of building a relationship based on trust and understanding is having some core knowledge about each other as people. Partners vary in the extent to which they know each other personally, and not every successful partnership becomes one of friendship. Nonetheless, partners will function more effectively if they have some information about each other's experiences, interests, and approaches. Also, some new teachers more than others feel the need to connect with their partners as people. Two exercises at the end of this chapter (3.1 and 3.2) provide quick and (we hope) enjoyable ways for you and your partner to share information about yourselves as people. In addition to these structured exercises, you will probably take advantage of informal opportunities to get to know each other as well. A lunchtime conversation over yogurt and a sandwich may be all the impetus you need to get the conversation rolling.

Getting to Know Each Other as Professionals

One principle of adult learning (Knowles, 1980, 1984) is that adults bring extensive life experiences that should be harvested to enhance new learning. Because many student teachers are young adults, their age may limit their life experiences; however, they usually have some foundation of experience because many student teachers have worked with children previously. And newly credentialed teachers have even more experience because they have been formally certified. Therefore, you can count on both kinds of partners to bring relevant experience and knowledge to the partnership.

If you have not done so yet, take a few minutes to ask about your partner's work with school-age children either in school settings or outside of school. Camp counseling, religious education, and day care experiences tend to be prevalent, even for young student teachers. Older adults are likely to bring the experience of parenthood, other careers, or life adventures that can enrich students' learning. When you recognize the attainments and capabilities of your new teacher partner, you send a strong message that you view your partner as a competent adult who is expanding the range of expertise to include classroom teaching. Additionally, this information can help you gauge the kind and amount of support that your partner may need through your work together.

Professionals in education tend to hold widely different views about the purposes of schooling, about how people learn, about what it means to teach well, and about how we should assess teaching and learning. Research in teacher cognition (e.g., Calderhead, 1991) suggests that many of these viewpoints are solidified before teachers even enter their initial teacher education programs. You may not have had the opportunity to think much about conceptions of education recently, so some exercises (3.3, 3.4, and 3.5 at the end of this chapter) may help you surface your thoughts. By taking time to examine views and experiences—your own and those of your partner—you can build shared goals. Knowing that you have similar—or dissimilar—views on human learning or discipline, for instance, can help you hold productive conversations about planning and teaching lessons.

Setting and Sharing Expectations

Expectations for cooperating teacher–student teacher relationships are different from new teacher–mentor expectations because the goals of the relationships are different. Variables include the evaluative function played by the experienced partner, the length of the relationship, the amount of the time partners spend together, and the intensity of their work.

In working with a student teacher, the more you agree on what is important and what needs to be accomplished during the term, the more likely you are to communicate well and to work toward shared goals. Initial explorations may begin with conversations with university personnel because it is critical that you understand your role in the teacher education program and find it compatible with your own views. Chapter 4 shares ideas for building a strong and productive relationship with the university supervisor. Information learned from the university supervisor can free you and your student teacher to devise a plan for your student teacher's classroom participation that is in harmony with the university's expectations and your own. It may also be helpful to use what you learned in the "getting to know each other as professionals" exercises to discuss your expectations for each other as professionals. Exercise 3.6 at the end of the chapter can provide another mechanism to talk about expectations and goals.

Work with a newly credentialed teacher will be shaped by the expectations of the induction or support program, by your view of the mentor role, and by the new teacher's views, past experiences, and goals. There is probably greater latitude for your work with your partner than the latitude allowed to student teacher–cooperating teacher pairs because you hold similar paid positions, despite the length of your experience and the level of your expertise. However, states across the nation vary widely in the specificity and nature of tasks they assign their mentors or support providers. To clarify expectations, check your job description. Read over documents that spell out the induction program's guidelines for your work with your partner. Jot down your questions and concerns, then be sure to get clarification from program leaders. Tell your partner any formal guidelines that require you to share information with others or that define confidentiality in your relationship. Which information will you hold as confidential? Which information might you share with others? In what form? Be frank about how your work with the new teacher is connected to the support and evaluation process led by the site administrator and district. Then, in the weeks that follow, diligently uphold the promises and expectations that you have agreed upon. Model your trustworthiness in every aspect of your professional duties because your new teacher will draw conclusions about his or her ability to trust you by observing how you protect the trust of others.

It can also be helpful for you to explicitly discuss what your partner can expect from you. Share your views of your role, and temper your views based on your partner's needs and hopes. Spend some time discussing goals, hopes, and concerns that the new teacher may hold at this point in your relationship. When expectations are clear, and shared, fewer guesses need to be made about how partners should behave.

BUILDING EFFECTIVE COMMUNICATION STRATEGIES

A trusting relationship is one key component of effective teacher partnerships. Effective communication is a second. Our own experience and research (e.g., Guillaume & Rudney, 2002) suggest to us that most novice–experienced teacher partnerships are successful. However, the potential for a teacher partnership to go awry looms large and, when relationships do go amiss, research (e.g., Connor & Killmer, 1995; Gotliffe, 1994; Wooley, 1997) and experience point to faulty or absent communication as a main contributing factor to troubled teacher partnerships.

Though it would seem easy for new and experienced teachers—all educated and typically articulate adults—to communicate clearly, several factors can interfere with successful communication. First, in the bustling atmosphere of the school, it is very easy to let communication assumptions go untested and expectations go unstated. It can be difficult to make the time to communicate clearly. Second, communicating with a novice professional can be awkward given the very different set of demands presented by this type of relationship. Some of the communication challenges presented for mentors include these six demands:

1. Adults are capable of—and demand—more complex kinds of communication than do children. You must converse at different levels, consider a wide range of topics, and use varied forms of communication all with an eye toward what is appropriate for the context at the moment.

2. Your new teacher partner is a novice, and novices in the same position can hold vastly different levels of competence. You will need to judge the skills and needs of your partner and communicate in ways that support your partner's autonomy while still providing the support that will help him or her move forward.

3. You will need to talk explicitly about your craft: teaching. A long line of research (beginning with Jackson, 1968) suggests that what teachers know often remains implicit. We ordinarily do not talk much about the art or skills of teaching, even with our colleagues. As a mentor or cooperating teacher, you work with someone who can benefit greatly if you are able and willing to discuss what you do when you teach.

4. You will need to assume roles that may compete. As a cooperating teacher, your first allegiance is to the students in your room. You will need to balance a novice's efforts with the students' best interests. You will need to help your student teacher acquire competence and confidence through modeling, by providing opportunities to practice, and by supplying feedback. You will also serve in a supportive role for your partner. Student teaching and first-year teaching are usually emotional experiences: learning to teach is important, demanding, difficult, and exhilarating. You have agreed to serve as the mentor who is there to console after the failed lessons and to celebrate after the successes.

5. The cooperating teaching role does not come without costs. Koerner (1992) documents the ambivalence of some cooperating teachers who wrestled with aspects of their role, such as sharing their students with another adult, the difficulty of being judged by another teacher, and the release of control over the curriculum and (to some degree) control of students' learning that come along with agreeing to take on a student teacher.

6. Finally, you will serve an evaluative function. Many states require their mentors or support providers to conduct formative (or ongoing) evaluation. As a cooperating teacher evaluating a student teacher's performance, the stakes are even higher. In completing a final assessment of the student teacher's competence, you address such questions as: Shall we entrust our children to this person? Is the granting of a credential warranted?

Perhaps it is partly the difficulty of achieving clear communication that makes new teachers prize it so highly. When we ask graduating student teachers what they

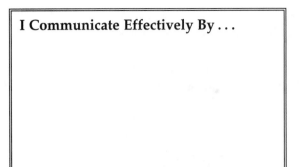

I Communicate Effectively By . . .

appreciated most from their cooperating teachers, they consistently place honest, forthright communication at the top of their list. In fact, when we recently asked student teachers for their cooperating teacher's most helpful and least helpful support strategies, communication (and poor or absent communication) topped both lists (Guillaume & Rudney, 2002). You, a professional educator, have clearly displayed competence in communicating, or you would not be in a position to read this book now. Which kinds of communication strategies do you use that will be effective in your partnership with your new teacher? Try jotting down a few notes in the textbox; then we can compare notes.

Active Listening

Active listening tops our list of effective communication strategies. Was it on yours? Active listening is the thread that can draw your faith in your partner into and through your everyday interactions and foster your commitment to your partner's growth.

Why Use Active Listening? A group of experienced teachers recently told us how difficult it is to be active listeners for their new teacher partners. Many laughed as they shared their tendencies to be "fixers" rather than "listeners." Their love of directing others and solving problems is partly what drew them to teaching. They also described the classroom context as a busy one with many demands and little time to reflect. These conditions can make it difficult to engage in active listening. But when mentors jump in to fix things, they might rob new teachers of the opportunity to thoroughly explore professional issues, make plans for action, and add to their knowledge and problem-solving abilities. By listening actively, the mentor conveys warmth, regard, genuine interest, and trust in the new teacher's ability to arrive at his or her own solutions.

How Do I Listen Actively? Prerequisite to active listening is the mindset of empathy, of appreciating your partner's perspective, experiences, and feelings while simultaneously remaining emotionally separate from them. Active listening involves three components: Physically attending to the message, mentally focusing on the message, and communicating one's understanding of the message.

1. *Physically attend:* Position your body so that your interest in the message is clear. Face-to-face positioning is effective in many cases. Stop multitasking and hold still. Use nonverbal cues such as eye contact, head nodding, or smiling to indicate that you are listening.

2. *Mentally focus:* Make your sole task for the moment that of understanding the message. Resist the temptation to formulate suggestions or share similar experiences of your own. Attend to messages that are being conveyed on two levels: verbal and nonverbal communications. Whereas *words* may give you the content of the message, *body language* may convey the speaker's emotions related to the message. An old German proverb holds that it is better to trust the eyes rather than the ears. Active listening requires you to trust both.

3. *Communicate understanding:* Check your reception of the message. For instance, rather than assuming that downcast eyes mean the speaker is rejecting your ideas, you

might say, "I notice you're looking down as we talk. I can't tell whether that means you're thinking, or whether it means something else." Some techniques for checking understanding include paraphrasing statements ("It sounds like you're worried about Period 5's respect for you."), clarifying questions ("Are you saying that . . .?"), and conveying your state of mind ("I'm not clear on . . . ."). Your check for understanding ensures that the message you heard was the message intended by the speaker. It also provides the speaker with an opportunity to refine his or her own thinking while giving form to ideas through words shared with an empathetic listener.

Ongoing Communication

Accepting a new teacher partner is, in one way, very much like accepting a spouse: it is continuous work to ensure that each person's needs are being expressed, valued, and met. In other ways, though, having a teacher partner is very different from having a spouse. You have a job to do with your new teacher partner, and that job will eventually come to an end. Further, that job is a bit one-sided. Though we know that support providers and cooperating teachers grow through their mentoring responsibilities, that is not the major goal of the partnership; the goal is new teacher success. For these reasons, your ongoing communications with your new teacher partner need to

- Assume a structure that is ongoing and relatively easy to maintain
- Use a variety of formats, including written and verbal, formal and informal
- Take into consideration the needs of the participants
- Be respectful and supportive
- Be honest
- Be nonthreatening (but explicit)

Box 3.1 gives some thoughts of successful student teachers that reflect these principles.

Box 3.1   Student Teachers' Thoughts on Clear Communication

- "What I appreciated was my cooperating teachers' honesty. Both semesters they asked about what I needed. I appreciated the feedback they gave me on what to improve."
- "It helped me that my cooperating teacher and I became friends. I trusted her completely and could ask her anything. She communicated openly."
- "I felt like a colleague because my cooperating teachers were open to learning and appreciated the ideas I brought to the classroom."
- "We used a journal to communicate openly, which we exchanged only every two or three days. Often it was easier to say things through writing. When I felt low, I looked back at days when I did well and took another look at praise from my cooperating teacher."
- "We set a date to meet during a certain hour each week. I was certain to ask my questions during our time for planning and talking, even if other times of the week were too busy."
- "Although I'm a night owl, it helped to 'become a morning person' for the semester in order to meet with my cooperating teacher during the time she was most open to talking: early, before-school hours."

These ideas suggest that structured communication, including a scheduled meeting time and a set format such as a dialogue journal, ensure that new teachers have opportunities to communicate with their experienced partners.

Chapter 7 discusses directive feedback in greater detail. The important idea to take away from this chapter is that successful communication between new and experienced teacher partners requires mutual understanding and partners' respect for each other as people and as professionals. It requires the adoption of at least one shared goal—the new teacher's growth—and requires commitments to honesty, openness, and support. When these conditions are met, new teachers and their experienced mentors are freed to focus on the important work of preparing the next generation of competent educators.

EXERCISES

Exercise 3.1   Uncommon Commonalties (adapted from Kagan, 1994)

In this exercise, you and your partner list as many commonalties as you can find in a three-minute period. Examples include, "We both like pizza with mushrooms but no olives," and "We both have traveled extensively within the United States." Listing such elements as, "We both call Earth home," or "We both are mammals" is less in keeping with the spirit of this activity.

1.   Time yourselves for three minutes. (Ignore the clock if you are not a rule follower, but having a goal adds a little pressure to keep the conversation moving.) Rely on your stream-of-conscious thinking to get you asking each other questions about things you may have in common. Hint: Start with appearance . . . color choice in clothes, for instance, if you need a push.

2.   The superstars in a group of cooperating teachers we recently worked with were two teachers who found 17 commonalties in three minutes. Can you beat the record? Keep your list and add to it over the term.

Exercise 3.2   Predictions

In this exercise, you and your partner make predictions about each other's tastes and experiences (adapted from Silberman, 1996).

1.   Look over the question list below. If the questions bore you, make up your own. You also need to make up your own questions if you and your partner already know each other.

2.   Decide who goes first. That person reads the question aloud, then makes a prediction. For example, a partner may say, "What is your all-time favorite song? It's clear to me that you are an 'Achy Breaky Heart' kind of person!" Do not be afraid to make bold, outlandish guesses. Next, the partner tells whether the prediction was accurate and elaborates before making a prediction on the same question for the partner.

Exercise 3.2   Continued

3.   Reflect: Were there lessons to be learned about judgments based upon limited experience and evidence? How could this activity be used in the classroom?

I predict . . .

What is your all-time favorite song?
What do you do for fun?
Are you a night owl or an early bird?
What is a typical breakfast for you?

Exercise 3.3   Discussion Starters

This activity provides charts for you and your partner to complete to spark discussion regarding your views on teaching.

1.   Choose one or more of the following charts. Prepare by making two copies of the charts you selected, or answer on other sheets.

2.   Complete the charts independently, then discuss your results. Ask each other questions that will help you gain a sense of each other's professional perspectives.

3.   Reflect: Did you find any surprises? How do your answers suggest different stages of professional development? How can you use this information to foster clear communication?

4.   Extend: These charts are adaptations of pre-reading activities to be used with elementary students (Yopp & Yopp, 1996). You no doubt have your own ideas that will work well with new teacher partners. Use your ideas to spark discussion. You may wish to try the discussion starters twice—at the beginning and end of the term—and compare your results on both occasions.

Anticipation Guide

Agree   Disagree

_____   _____   1. The purpose of education is to teach people skills.

_____   _____   2. The purpose of education is to teach people enduring ideas from the classic fields of study.

_____   _____   3. The purpose of education is to help people develop as individuals.

_____   _____   4. The purpose of education is to help individuals learn to act toward the common good.

Opinionnaire/Questionnaire

1. What words best describe a good teacher? (Option: Rank your selections and add a couple of your own words in the blanks provided.)

___ Loving   ___ Intelligent   ___ Serious   ___ Mean   ___ Old

___ Enthusiastic   ___ Organized   ___ Consistent   ___ Thoughtful   ___ Young

___ Funny   ___ Crazy   ___ Trained   ___ Calm   ___ Flexible

___ Female   ___ Male   ___ Political   ___ _____   ___ _____

2. How do you think someone becomes a good teacher?

___ She takes classes and studies.   ___ He thinks about his teaching.

___ She is born that way.   ___ He learns how to maintain discipline.

___ She has years of experience.   ___ He does not smile until the holidays.

___ _____   ___ _____

3. How would you know a good teacher when you saw one?

___ The class would be quiet.   ___ The students would look interested.

___ The class would be noisy.   ___ The students would think of their

___ The class would be neat.   teacher as a friend.

___ The class would be messy.   ___ The students would think of their teacher as a higher being.

___ _____   ___ _____

Contrast Chart

	On a Nightmare Day	On a Wonderful Dream Day
I, as the teacher, would . . .		
The students would . . .		
The lessons would . . .		
The weather would . . .		

Exercise 3.4 I Need/I Like Statements

This activity invites you to explore and discuss elements that are necessary to you as a classroom teacher and elements that are merely nice (adapted from Charles, 1996).

1. You and your partner prepare by each making a chart with three boxes: I need, I like, I dislike. See the sample below:

I Need	
I Like	
I Dislike	

2. Complete the charts individually, then compare your results.
3. Reflect: Compare your charts. What will you do about the differences?
4. Extend: Try comparing your lists to what you perceive as the "typical" answer at your site. Think about whether or how your needs and likes have changed with experience.

Sample I Need/I Like Statements

I Need	• for students to treat each other (and me) with respect and compassion. • an organized environment so that the teacher and students together have the freedom to explore without having to worry about routines. • freedom as a professional to select content, pedagogy, and scheduling to best meet my students' needs.
I Like	• humor. • natural consequences. • students to exercise initiative to get their needs met. • a sense of community and interest that ties me to my students.
I Dislike	• helping students become less dependent upon the teacher for praise and sanction. (It is difficult!) • approaches that demean students or do not consider their perspectives.

Exercise 3.5   Metaphors for Teaching

Through this activity you and your partner develop analogies that capture critical aspects of your teaching. Developing analogies is a creative activity, so skip this exercise if open-ended explorations do not appeal to you.

1.   Think about commonly identified metaphors, including teacher as sculptor, gardener, actor, or guide. Teachers we know have compared teachers and classrooms to jugglers, amusement parks, and field shows. Maxine Greene's (1973) famous metaphor is *Teacher as Stranger*.

2.   In a foil sculpture, in writing, or in a picture or diagram, capture your own analogy for teaching. It may help to start by asking yourself: What is teaching like? What is a teacher like? What are students like? What is the curriculum like?

3.   Compare your metaphor with your that of your partner. How do they compare in their treatment of the student, teacher, and curriculum? You may want to think about the dimensions of active versus passive, of certain versus unpredictable.

4.   Reflect: What might be the implications of your different (or similar) views in how you talk about teaching and learning?

5.   Extend: Analyze your own metaphor: Which aspects of teaching seem clearer as a result of the analogy? Where does the metaphor seem to break down?

Exercise 3.6   Knowledge Chart: Setting Goals for the Term

Know-Want-Learned (K-W-L) charts (Ogle, 1986) are a popular strategy for developing active reading of expository text. This activity uses a K-W-L chart to help you select goals for your mentoring relationship with your new teacher partner. Use the chart to explore what your new teacher partner knows and wants to learn about teaching. Later, review by completing the "L" (learned) column.

1.   Create a K-W-L chart similar to the one found below.

2.   Complete the chart together through supportive conversation. Choose the open format or the one with domains listed for a bit more direction. In the "K" column, record what your teacher partner already *Knows*. It may help to ask what was studied in the methods courses or what opportunities were provided in a previous student teaching (or other) setting. Record your own knowledge if it helps build the team, but you may wish to include your entries in another color or initial them so that you remember whose are whose. In the "W" column include questions or topics that your student teacher *Wants* to learn. Be patient for these questions. They may be slow in coming. At the close of the term (or in an ongoing manner), reflect on the chart by adding to the "L" or *Learned* column.

3.   Refer to the chart throughout the term, adding important insights over time.

4.   Reflect: At the close of the term, add another column. Choose "A" for affect (record feelings related to the knowledge and questions) or another "W" for what your new teacher partner wants to learn next.

Sample Open-Ended K-W-L Chart

Know	*Want*	*Learned*

K-W-L Chart With Suggested Domains of Teaching
(Substitute your own if you like)

	Know	*Want*	*Learned*
Discipline & Management			
Subject Matter			
Planning			
Instruction			

	Know	Want	Learned
Assessment			
Reaching All Learners			
Professional Development			

4

University Supervision: The Triad

"We have such a good relationship with the university. They're a part of us when they walk in the door."

—An experienced cooperating teacher

In Chapter 3, you read about the importance of building a successful relationship with your student teacher. Now we invite into the picture an important third person, who connects field experiences to the overall program. A representative from the university, often called the *university supervisor*—or simply *supervisor*—will work to assist you and your student teacher to meet and assess the goals of the student teaching experience. Though we have heard of instances where the university supervisor was regrettably viewed as a "snoopervisor," we know that in fact this person can provide invaluable expertise and support to you and your student teacher. The three of you are the *triad* and, in this chapter, you will read about how to get the most out of this supervision team. (If you are a mentor, please take note of the following "Note to Mentors" textbox.)

To start, complete Table 4.1. What commonalities and differences do you find for the members of the triad?

Building on commonalities is one of the keys to successful partnerships. Recognizing the special advantages to differences in perspective or experience is another important factor. Let's examine the advantageous—but sometimes tricky—life inside the supervision triad.

Table 4.1   Triad Members' Commonalities and Differences

	Cooperating Teacher	Student Teacher	University Supervisor
Goals for Student Teaching			
Contributions			
Things to Learn			

Note to Mentors

Mentor, much of this chapter applies to experienced teachers whose partners are under the direct supervision of the university through its supervisors. Whether or not you are connected to a university program in your current role, similar dynamics may exist. We hope you find the chapter useful to you. Some interesting food for thought:

- *Intern teachers* (those still enrolled in a university program) reported that they would go first to their university advisor if they had a serious problem (Tellez, 1992).
- *Novice teachers* (those in their first and second years of teaching) appreciated and learned from their school mentors but did not always feel *safe* to vary in style or strategies. Support from district mentors *and* university partners was valued (Chubbuck, Clift, Allard, & Quinlan, 2001)

"WHO IS THAT PERSON AND WHY IS SHE HERE?"

The university supervisor who works with you will have had successful classroom experience, though not necessarily in your grade level or subject area. Those who meet high standards of the National Council for the Accreditation of Teacher Education (NCATE) will have been selected and prepared for their supervisory role and will have the skills, knowledge, and

> "Any supervisor worth his salt would rather deal with people who attempt to do much than with those who try too little."
>
> —Lee Iacocca
> (quoted in Creative Quotations, 2002)

dispositions of highly accomplished professionals (NCATE, 2001). (By the way, NCATE's target level holds *cooperating teachers* to the identical standard!)

Specific experiences, training, perspectives, and expectations vary and depend upon the nature and structure of the university's teacher education program. Some supervisors are tenured faculty who participate fully in university-based as well as field-based programs. Others are graduate students completing masters or doctoral programs. Still others may be adjunct faculty who may or may not have a close connection to the coursework or other preparation activities. Each *type* of supervisor, as well as each *individual* supervisor, will bring different strengths and limitations to the experience.

University supervisors traditionally have three main responsibilities. First, they assist and evaluate student teachers. Usually, they observe and conduct follow-up conferences for several lessons, review planning documentation, and read journals and other reflective assignments. They listen to student teachers' ideas and concerns, make suggestions, and give feedback. As part of their evaluation, they complete observation records, write lesson evaluations, record anecdotal evidence, and prepare final evaluations. To make sure that a student teacher is meeting all program standards and requirements, they consult carefully with the cooperating teacher.

They also have the responsibility to support each cooperating teacher's work with his or her individual student teacher. You can expect them to communicate regularly, explain program procedures and expectations, and respond to questions and concerns. They can answer questions about the program, supervision strategies, typical student-teacher behavior and progress, and your student teacher's specific progress and skill level.

Finally, university supervisors serve as liaisons between the school and college, interacting with university personnel, school administrators, and all those involved in the student teaching process. If the program they represent adheres to the highest teacher education standards, they will solicit your ideas and input for program improvement. NCATE (2001), for example, expects accredited institutions to show that field experiences and clinical practice are characterized by collaboration between the institution and school partners. This collaboration includes the design and implementation of field experiences, assessment of candidate performance, and selection of cooperating teachers and mentors. Your ideas are important!

University supervisors can contribute significantly to the student teaching experience as a complement to the active engagement of cooperating and student teachers. They are particularly successful at providing information, keeping things running, and making connections between theory and practice (Slick, 1997; Wilson & Saleh, 2000). As one cooperating teacher explains,

> One of their key jobs for my benefit is to keep reminding me that the student teachers are *practicing* to become teachers . . . . I keep expecting so much from them. The supervisor comes in and says, "How are they *growing* to become a teacher?" It takes me back to the proper plane.

Their vantage point allows university supervisors to see many student teachers and offers a comparative element to the supervision process. Table 4.2 summarizes the complementary perspectives of the field-based and university-based teacher educators.

UNDERSTANDING THE ESSENTIALS OF THE SUPERVISION TRIAD

Despite its positive attributes, the traditional model of supervision is not trouble free. Exploration of essential themes found in the shared supervision process will uncover both the pitfalls and promise of working together to prepare and support beginning teachers. As you read about the essential themes, notice that we see *sharing* as the key to success.

Sharing Goals and Appreciating Perspectives

The best way to begin your work with the university supervisor is for you both to think about your goals for the student teaching experience. How do you answer these questions?

- What is your main goal as cooperating teacher?
- How do you think you should meet that goal?

Compare your answers to those of an experienced cooperating teacher who says that the relationship benefits both parties:

I think the main goal for me is to give some of the knowledge that I've gained back to the university through my experiences. I try to make it just a little easier transition for the student teachers when they get into the workforce. I love to give them little tips and ideas that have worked for me.

We love having practicum students because it gives *us* ideas. We see our student teachers trying new strategies and developing new units and say to ourselves, "Oh that's right—we could be doing that!" It definitely works both ways. I'm definitely looking for ideas from the student teachers *and* looking to share with them the best of what I know.

Table 4.2   Perspectives of Those Who Mentor Preservice and Beginning Teachers

Feature	*Cooperating Teacher*	*University Supervisor*
Focus	Classroom events and students	Programmatic processes and student teachers
Priorities	First: Own pupils' learning Second: Student teacher's learning	First: Student teachers' learning Second: K-12 student learning
Special Expertise	Grade level and subject area curriculum, instruction, and pupil characteristics; school and community context; individual pupils in classroom	State and national teacher education standards and licensure information; institutional context; adult learning
Scope	Specific and extensive knowledge of own classroom, own pupils, and own student teacher	General knowledge of many classrooms, many pupils, and many student teachers
Professional Concerns	Balancing the need to give the student teacher a chance to experiment and learn from mistakes with the need to ensure quality learning experiences for own pupils	Balancing the need to support and encourage the student teacher and cooperating teacher with the need to ensure that program standards are met
Qualifications	Licensed, tenured teachers; high standards require that they have participated in training for supervision	Academically prepared and professionally experienced in the school setting; high standards require that they have contemporary professional experiences in school settings at the levels they supervise.

Box 4.1   Building Alliances With Supervisors

- "Share and compare goals. Think about ways to work together so that all goals are met."
- "Share and compare ideas of 'best' classroom practice."
- "Invite the supervisor to teach a lesson to your students."
- "Ask for explanations of the program and expectations. Listen carefully and remember."
- "Provide information about your classroom to help establish a context for observation."
- "Show an interest in their findings and interpretations of a lesson observation."
- "Ask how the student teacher compares with others."
- "Offer suggestions and constructive criticism to improve the program."
- "Talk often."

And here are the comments of another experienced cooperating teacher:

I want to give the student teachers some practice teaching. I always try to give them as much time in front of the classroom as they seem to be ready for. . . . That's the best way for them to see how it really feels to teach. I want to help them work through things. . . . I think one of the most difficult things for new teachers is that realization of how hard it is to manage a classroom—the discipline, the time management. When they do teach a lesson, I want to give them time to reflect and time to talk with me about how to do the lesson better. Then I want to give them the experience of being able to practice again.

For comparison, here is the perspective of an experienced university supervisor:

I think about this whole idea of development. I want to see them [the student teachers] grow, and I want to facilitate that growth in some way. I want to look at all of the student teachers individually, where they are in terms of subject matter and pedagogy, but also their feelings about teaching, their disposition. I guess that's what I want—to facilitate their growth, to help them be the best teachers that they can. The other goal is to somehow help the cooperating teachers, to make them comfortable enough to come to me with any problem. I'm the one that should be there helping both the student teacher and the cooperating teacher. One of my goals is to be a public relations person between the university and the school. That's a big part of being the university supervisor . . . because we want the relationship to continue the next year. It's not a simple answer.

You can see that excellent field-based and university-based educators care deeply about the process and recognize the complexities of teaching and of their role in helping others learn to teach. Notice how perspectives toward practice, reflection, facilitation, support, and communication are present in the comments. We recommend that you share and understand the goals you and your supervisory partner have for the field experience. Box 4.1 provides

---

Box 4.2   Helpful Hints for Working Well With the University Supervisor

---

From cooperating teachers:

- "Build a strong relationship with the university supervisor before the student teacher comes."

- "Feel free to say, 'This isn't working; we need to do something.'"

- "If the student teacher doesn't introduce the supervisor, be sure to do it. I try to tell my student teacher before the visit that it's important for the students to know who the supervisor is."

- "Find out where else the university supervisors are going and what else they're doing. It helps me to know how busy they are so I know what to expect . . . . The more information we know about the supervisor's responsibilities, the easier it is for us."

- "Encourage the supervisors to become a part of the classroom for however long they are there. By talking with one or two of the students, they will get a better sense of what's going on."

- "Take the supervisor's requirements seriously. Even though I think the actual teaching experience is what teaches the student teacher the most about the actual experience of teaching, I still think that the things that are required—like lesson plans and objectives and teaching philosophies—are important. That foundation is important."

- "Ask questions."

From university supervisors:

- "Believe that the decisions I make are because I want the student teacher to become the best possible teacher for his future students."

- "Be open with your concerns about what is going on in the classroom. Have consistent communication. Be open and willing to share."

- "Try to make time in your busy day to meet with me when I come. Sit down with me and the student teacher."

- "Introduce me to all the teachers who are involved with the student teacher. Help me understand the system the school has set up for that grade."

- "Let me know the student teacher's strengths (as well as your concerns) so they can be evaluated appropriately."

- "Let me know if there is any way that I can assist you."

---

other suggestions for building a relationship with the university supervisor. Compare them with the advice other cooperating teachers and university supervisors offer in Box 4.2. You will see commonalities and unique ideas in the lists.

> "The world changes according to the way people see it, and if you alter, even by a millimeter, the way . . . people look at reality, then you can change it."
>
> —James Baldwin
> (quoted in Creative Quotations, 2002)

Sometimes, though goals are similar, there seems to be a clash in perspective. Cooperating teachers may question the validity of supervisors' comments because the supervisors are not working in the "real world" (Veal & Rikard, 1998). The clash in perspective between school and university is often described as a difference between theory and practice. Once, in a triad meeting, we listened to a cooperating teacher say, "Real teachers don't do all these plans. They're just making you jump through hoops." Comments like these are sometimes made in an attempt to comfort the student teacher, and you may believe them. Unfortunately, the view and the comment are not helpful to the supervision and learning process and may undermine the potential good that will come from the supervisor. Successful cooperating teachers understand that assignments are purposeful and linked to the university faculty's desire to prepare excellent teachers. Often assignments help students sharpen necessary skills or reflections. And they are usually necessary for defensible assessment decisions. It is true that many experienced teachers do not write detailed lesson plans for each lesson taught in a day, but consider this: When you want a difficult lesson or concept to go well, what do you do? The answer for most of us is that we create a plan. Also remember that, because you are an expert, you may have so assimilated theory into your practice that you may be unaware of the principles that support your teaching.

Sadly, there are also stories of university supervisors whose comments may undermine the work of cooperating teachers. Focused on the *ideals* of best practice, some may miss what Winograd (1998) calls the "in-your-face" realities of classroom life. In the story of his brief return to the classroom, he describes his realization that theory—as he teaches it at the university—is easier to articulate than to implement. He adds, however, that the usefulness of theory increases as it interacts with practice. He suggests looking for "middle ground, common spaces, and, perhaps, the inevitability of trade-offs reflected in most solutions" (Winograd, 1998, p. 305).

When partners collaborate to link preparation and practice, both sets of experiences improve (Weaver & Stanulis, 1996). What are some ways to build middle ground and common spaces? The ideas that top our list are open communication, intentional invitations to participate in your classroom, and holding expectations that your experience and expertise are valued.

Sharing Space and Power

So far in this chapter, we have looked at two people in the supervision triad—you and the university representative. Of course, there are *three* adult participants involved, and each one brings unique perspectives, strengths, and areas of potential growth. One of the main problems with the triad is one that is not unique to supervision of student teachers; rather, it is a function of human dynamics. With groups of three, someone is often left out. Do you have a sense of who that usually is when it comes to the supervision triad? If you think it is the university supervisor, you are right.

The cooperating teacher and student teacher are together on a daily basis and develop a powerful dyad. This dyad is rich with time and presence—two key factors in any relationship. Cooperating teachers, because they interact with their student teachers many times every day, are most accessible and able to provide help, feedback, ideas, and encouragement. Especially when things are going well in the classroom, it is a strong relationship that can have a great impact on the student teacher's development. This powerful dyad is susceptible to disturbance when a third member, the university supervisor, enters the picture (Veal & Rikard, 1998).

The university supervisor's arrival creates two additional dyads. Both are affected by the context of the school, teacher education program, and specific expectations of and for the supervisor. Earlier in this chapter, we described elements of the dyad formed by the cooperating teacher and supervisor. This dyad, when functioning well, provides incredible support for the student teacher. When roles are clearly defined, the supervisory dyad will enhance the growth and development of the student teacher (Slick, 1997).

The third dyad, formed by the university supervisor and student teacher, is dependent upon previous interaction and experience. If the supervisor has many student teachers and little connection to prior experience, relationship building must start from scratch. In programs where the same individual serves both as the university-based instructor and the field-based supervisor, the student teacher and university supervisor have a well-established relationship that allows the supervisor greater opportunity to make significant contributions.

Who has the power? This is a most interesting aspect of the supervision triad to analyze. The power structure within the triad—or the multiple dyads—is a very real and influential dynamic. Often, the cooperating teacher seems to assume—or to be assigned—a subservient

> "As you enter positions of trust and power, dream a little before you think."
>
> —Toni Morrison
> (quoted in Creative Quotations, 2002)

role (Daane, 2000). Some cooperating teachers report that university supervisors do not seem to respect the efforts, routine, and other elements of their classrooms. These teachers wonder about their supervisory role and perceive that they are simply told what to do. Feeling powerless, they need more information and are frustrated that the university fails to provide clear and explicit expectations and, in fact, gives conflicting, unclear directives and goals (Koerner, 1992).

In contrast to their perceived lack of power, cooperating teachers *do* influence their student teachers' learning and have a strong immediate impact on their performance (Kauffman, 1992). University supervisors recognize this and at times struggle with their own *limited* impact. In an assignment for a graduate course in supervision, one supervisor wrote about cooperating teachers:

> I have long recognized their power in shaping the behavior of student teachers. So often my student teachers have found meaning in what I said or demonstrated in class only if they could see it in the activities of their cooperating teachers.

Though university supervisors often have planning and decision-making power, they also can harbor feelings of frustration similar to their school-based colleagues. Just as the cooperating teachers struggle with multiple responsibilities and not enough time to manage them, supervisors juggle competing and multiple demands. A real confusion for some supervisors is their role at the university where, especially at large research institutions, there may be a schism between the clinical faculty who teach and supervise preservice teachers, and the tenure-line professors who concentrate more on graduate students and scholarship (Bullough, Hobbs, Kauchak, Crow, & Stokes, 1997). Program expectations may be unclear (Slick, 1998a), and some university supervisors are disturbed by the fact that they may be supervising in a field or grade level in which they have little experience (Borko & Mayfield, 1995). Supervisors can feel that they are outsiders both in the schools and at the university (Fulwiler, 1996; Slick, 1998b).

Student teachers are also part of the struggle. They often report feeling torn between two points of view: the perceived or actual differences between your expectations and those of the university supervisor. They need much support and, when the triad is functioning well, they receive it both from the cooperating teachers and the university supervisors.

Despite tensions, a successful three-way partnership strives for collegiality, negotiation, and shared experience (Weaver & Stanulis, 1996), and we know that it is possible. What ideas do you already have for sharing space and power? Try "sharing space" by understanding schedules, preparing your students, and planning for classroom visits from the supervisor. Invite the supervisor to teach a lesson. Share power by clarifying your expected responsibilities and rights within the program. Seek assistance and expect support. Provide information about your classroom that will help the university supervisor interpret the student teacher's performance. Talk often. The more cooperating teachers, supervisors, and student teachers understand, the better they can work together and learn from each other.

Sharing Time and Effort

> "All human power is a compound of time and patience."
>
> —Honore de Balzac
> (quoted in Creative Quotations, 2002)

Time is on *your* side. One of the most important factors that affects the student teacher is the amount of time the teacher educator is present. That, of course, is an advantage to you, the cooperating teacher. You are the one who sees the most and therefore are most available for support and instruction (Daane, 2000; Wilson & Saleh, 2000). You have the most in-depth knowledge of your student teacher's day-to-day pattern of planning, behaviors, and interactions.

Sometimes you or the student teacher may question the accuracy of a supervisor's evaluation because she was only in the classroom for an hour or two. This highlights a problem of logistics. There is no way a supervisor can be in one particular classroom all of the time, and everyone feels the effects. Despite time limitations, experienced supervisors have extensive knowledge of student teachers in general and may have individual knowledge of a particular student teacher due to prior experiences. They also learn much about each student teacher—even with limited time—from the numerous materials they are required to review. What Borko and Mayfield (1995) call "paperwork" is a rich source of information for the university supervisors. The review of journals, lesson plans, and observation notes provides fodder for useful discussions with student teachers and cooperating teachers.

A load shared is a load lightened. Depending on how well your student teacher is progressing, the amount of support you need will vary. This cooperating teacher captures the shifting needs:

The [first] student teachers were good and enthusiastic. I didn't have a lot of contact except when the supervisor came out to observe. It was generally a matter of sharing positive information. With one student teacher, I had a great deal of difficulty.

She was not meeting expectations, and I was not sure really where to go. The university supervisor really helped because that was where I was able to turn and say, "Here's what's happening. What should I do? Okay. I've done that. Now what?" I got a lot of support. In the end, I knew that I had done as much as I could to help the student teacher develop into a teacher.

Cooperating teachers who have good relationships with the university supervisors with whom they work especially appreciate their expertise in assessment. In programs where the responsibility for the student teaching experience lies almost completely with the cooperating teachers, they have struggled most

> "Great discoveries and improvements invariably involve the cooperation of many minds."
>
> —Alexander Graham Bell
> (quoted in Creative Quotations, 2002)

with grading and evaluation (Daane, 2000). In one study cooperating teachers and supervisors alike preferred a shared evaluation—with university supervisors assuming the greater responsibility (Zheng & Webb, 2000). When student teachers are having serious problems, the university supervisor also will assume important leadership and support roles. Chapter 9 addresses that difficult—and rare—situation.

Research has indicated that success in student teaching relates to the support provided both by cooperating teachers and university supervisors, especially when they work together to guide the student teachers' growth by challenging existing beliefs and modeling both thinking and action (Borko & Mayfield, 1995). The student teacher as part of the team both learns from and teaches his or her two mentors.

CONTEXT FOR COMMUNICATION AND COLLABORATION

The details of your experience will depend on the nature of the teacher education program. Much of what we have described for successful work in the supervision triad is based on *one* triad and, as you can see, much can be accomplished on that level. Collaboration—among groups of student teachers, cooperating teachers, and supervisors—also has advantages. Many teacher education programs follow a center school model where several student teachers are placed at a single site. Clustering student teachers at a school has many benefits, including increased opportunities for collaboration, formal and informal support, and workshops or seminars for all members of the triads. The university supervisor, able to focus more time at a single location, can increase his or her support and teaching for student teachers and for cooperating teachers.

The most complex collaborative effort is the Professional Development School (PDS). PDSs show promise for preservice teacher growth and development because they are designed to share power, expertise, and responsibilities (Winitzky, Stoddart, & O'Keefe, 1992). Rice (2002) explains that PDSs may be difficult to sustain because of the necessary funding, multiple commitments, and formalized structure. Stressing the importance of communication and collaboration, Rice explains that one of the key factors in the success of a PDS is the prior relationships established among the participants. And thus we return to the beginning and the importance of your relationship with *your* student teacher, *your* university supervisor and, of course, *your* students. We hope the exercises that follow are useful to you as you organize thoughts and materials to successfully work in the supervision triad.

EXERCISES

Exercise 4.1   Understanding Expectations

Be proactive in understanding the expectations of the program and the help you can expect to receive from the university representative. We have listed questions that many cooperating teachers have asked, and we have left room for your own. Study the program materials that you have received from your student teacher's institution to see if they answer your questions. If they do not, ask the supervisor, student teacher, or knowledgeable others. (Exercise 4.2 will help you keep track of the questions and answers.)

Questions and Concerns	What the Materials Say	My Thoughts
How often should I observe my student teacher?		
How often will the supervisor come to my classroom?		
How often can I expect to meet with the supervisor?		
What should I do if the student teacher is having problems?		
What if I don't understand some of the assignments?		
What information about my classroom would be helpful for the supervisor to know?		

Exercise 4.2   Preparing for a Supervision Conference

As an experienced teacher, you already know the steps involved in a good parent conference. Many of the same principles apply to supervision conferences. You want the time together to result in the sharing of information. You want to give information and receive clarification and support. You want to set goals, implementation plans, and assessments. The following chart has plenty of room for you to organize your thoughts, concerns, and ideas.

Preparation	Response/Plan	Follow-Up
Questions I (or we) have:		
Information to share:		
Concerns:		

Exercise 4.3 Rating the University Supervisor, Part 1

The following list of responsibilities, adapted from the Elementary Education Program Handbook at the University of Minnesota-Morris (University of Minnesota-Morris Teacher Education, 2002), represents typical expectations for university supervisors. For each, rate its level of importance to you and the supervisor's level of accomplishment. (We include a rating scale, but you can use any one that works for you.)

Supervisor Responsibilities	*Importance (1 = not at all and 3 = very)*	*Accomplishment (1 = needs work and 3 = great)*
Serve as a liaison between university and school.		
Meet with school administrators.		
Provide information about program expectations and requirements.		
Address questions and concerns.		
Monitor placements carefully.		
Solicit feedback and suggestions for program improvement.		
Seek to understand the social and cultural context of the school.		
Assist the cooperating teacher.		
Meet regularly throughout the student teaching experience.		
Answer questions and clarify information.		
Confer with cooperating teacher about student teacher progress.		
Conference with the student teacher and cooperating teacher at the midpoint and conclusion of the experience and other times when needed.		
Seek to understand the special needs and features of the classroom.		

Supervisor Responsibilities	Importance (1 = not at all and 3 = very)	Accomplishment (1 = needs work and 3 = great)
Solicit feedback and suggestions for program and supervisory improvement.		
If student teacher exhibits behaviors that cause concern, work with the cooperating teacher to determine, implement, and evaluate corrections.		
Schedule observations and conferences with consideration for the needs of the classroom.		
Suggest and share resources.		
Assist the student teacher.		
Meet prior to the experience to explain and clarify information.		
Meet early in the experience to clarify procedures and answer questions.		
Make at least four scheduled observations that include pre- and post-observation conferences.		
Encourage student teacher reflection		
Read and respond to journals, plans, and other assignments.		
Be specific when giving feedback.		
Build on strengths.		
Suggest and share resources.		
Other—Add anything we missed, and please let us know if there's something we should add!		

Exercise 4.4 Rating the University Supervisor, Part 2

Analyze the levels of importance and the ratings you gave the university supervisor in Exercise 4.3 and use the results to enhance the productivity and success of your relationship. The following table may be helpful.

Possible Findings	Suggested Actions	Your Ideas
Every item in both columns received top marks.	Celebrate! The program is great and the supervisor is terrific.	
Supervisor ratings mostly high; importance levels mixed or mostly low.	Show the chart to the supervisor and seek clarification. Seek to understand the rationale for responsibilities and requirements. Make specific suggestions.	
Both columns show mixed ratings. Supervisor received high ratings for items you rated as important.	Give positive feedback and continue to communicate your ideas and suggestions.	
Both columns show mixed ratings. You have concerns about supervisor's performance on key responsibilities.	Schedule a conference as soon as possible. Ask for clarification on each responsibility so that all members of the triad know expectations. Give specific statements of your need for communication. Focus on common goals. **Most problems will be resolved with clear communication, but if not:** • Analyze the concern from the point of view of the student teacher. To what degree do any of your concerns affect his or her learning or evaluation? • Continue to communicate interest and concerns to the supervisor. • Speak professionally about the supervisor as you solicit advice and assistance from your building administrator or university program directors.	

Exercise 4.5 Rating Yourself

Fair is fair! Rate the level of importance to you and your level of accomplishment on each of the following tips for successful cooperating teachers. Look also at other ideas shared in later chapters. Think about ways that you can improve your performance in the areas you believe are the most important. Thanks for being open to self-evaluation!

Supervisor Responsibilities	Importance (1 = not at all and 3 = very)	Accomplishment (1 = needs work and 3 = great)
Help the student teacher make connections between the theoretical foundations and practical application of the education knowledge base.		
Assist the student teacher in reflecting on his or her student teaching experience.		
Encourage the student teacher to share thoughts and concerns. Interpret them based on models of teacher development and individual needs.		
Encourage the student teacher to try new lesson strategies and ideas.		
Establish and maintain a collaborative relationship with the student teacher and the university supervisor.		
Communicate with the university supervisor and the student teacher throughout the student teaching experience.		
Read and understand program materials. Ask the supervisor if there are questions.		
Share resource materials and ideas with the student teacher.		
Share resource materials and ideas with the university supervisor.		
Explain important information about your classroom to the university supervisor.		
Answer questions professionally and accurately.		
Other—Add anything we missed, and please let us know if there's something we should add!		

Off and Running

The First Week

"Whoa! Hold everything!"

—Many new teachers

Student teachers and new teachers sometimes feel that they leap onto the classroom merry-go-round while it is already spinning. Lots of things happen in classrooms, they happen quickly, and they happen in ways unique to the individual school, teacher, and students. It can be difficult for the novice to hop aboard. Even when the new teacher or student teacher is present at the beginning of the year or term, there is much to learn.

The first week has tremendous potential to fuel your new teacher's success, and many of the factors that relate to your new partner's success are under your direct control. You can carefully structure opportunities to maximize chances for a healthy relationship and a successful experience.

> "Before beginning, plan carefully."
>
> —Marcus Tullius Cicero
> (quoted in Creative Quotations, 2002)

This chapter's goal is to provide guidelines and suggestions for using the critical first week of the partnership to build toward a successful experience. The chapter is organized into four parts that can help you and your new teacher partner take off . . . and run:

1. Using the First Week to Build Your Relationship

2. Building Communication Structures

3. Planning the Student Teaching Experience

4. Becoming Familiar with the Students, Classroom, School, and Local Context

(Note: This chapter makes many suggestions. They are summarized in Exercise 5.1 with space for your notes.)

USING THE FIRST WEEK TO BUILD YOUR RELATIONSHIP

The first week of your relationship with your new teacher provides a powerful opportunity for you to build your relationship with your partner. Though there are many commonalties between two kinds of mentoring relationships (cooperating teacher–student teacher and support provider–new teacher), there are important differences.

Building Trust With the Student Teacher

You can display your faith in your student teacher's capacity to succeed by mentally, physically, and professionally making him or her a presence in your classroom. The student teacher's professional presence can be recognized in your room in a few simple ways:

- Carve out a workspace for the student teacher in your classroom. Give your partner a place to put his or her things and to work. Be careful of the implicit message sent by the size and location of the workspace. (Do you have a "commander's bridge," while your student teacher has a tiny desk in a far, dark corner of the room? Alternatively, does placing the desks across the room from each other convey the message that power is balanced, with a teacher for each half of the room?)

- Consider giving your partner a small gift that represents your commitment to the relationship and the student teacher's entry into the profession. Gifts can convey powerful symbolism, even if they are just tokens. Box 5.1 cites examples of gifts that cooperating teachers recently reported giving to their student teachers.

- Post your student teacher's name as you post your own. Is your name on the door? Add your student teacher's name. Include a welcome message on the board.

- Formally welcome the student teacher to your students and their parents. Allow the student teacher to share a PowerPoint presentation on his or her background and interests, or extend a warm welcome in the newsletter or in a separate letter to students' homes. Include mention of your student teacher's professional experiences and the strengths he or she brings to your classroom. Or, invite the student teacher to write his or her own letter of introduction and read it over before the student teacher sends it to students' homes.

- Use language that presents the student teacher as a colleague rather than as an aid or assistant. We know a school where student teachers are referred to as "associate teachers," for instance. Student teachers are often in the early stages of establishing themselves as authority figures, and your careful use of words with parents and students can support your partner's efforts to establish authority with the students.

Box 5.1   Examples of Gifts to Student Teachers From Cooperating Teachers

---

- Photo book with individual shots of the students, or instant or digital class shots with students labeled
- A professional book on classroom management or another pertinent issue
- A teacher mug
- A welcome basket with seating charts, the photocopy machine code number, office supplies, and a bit of chocolate
- A plan book that matches that of the cooperating teacher
- A disposable camera for documenting other teachers' great room environment ideas, or for capturing the student teacher working with students (photos are great for professional portfolios!)

You can also display your confidence in your partner's competence by immediately recognizing his or her prior life and professional experiences and by ensuring that the student teacher sees you as a fellow learner who plans to grow through this experience. Student teachers and cooperating teachers have shared with us some strategies they found to be helpful in establishing a collegial relationship:

- The cooperating teacher sits with the student teacher at faculty meetings, lunch, and other events and makes introductions to the staff and administration.
- The cooperating teacher openly discusses and models the perspective that mistakes are a natural, healthy part of the learning process and that reflection allows professionals to grow from their mistakes.
- The student teacher considers the cooperating teacher not just an instructional model but also a person with whom to discuss and reflect on the decisions that go into every moment of teaching.

Clearly, trust between you and your student teacher will develop over time as you gain a clearer sense of each other as people and as professionals, but actively displaying—from the very first day—your faith in your partner's ability to succeed can do much to establish a strong footing for that growing trust.

Building Trust With the New Teacher Partner

Some of the trust-building strategies we suggest in the previous section can be effective for building trust with new teacher partners as well. However, because the relationship between a new teacher and a support provider is different from that between a student teacher and cooperating teacher, trust building can be a bit different. Given the length of the relationship (one or two years rather than just a couple months), trusting relationships can often unfold unhurriedly over time. You can, nonetheless, take overt actions from the very first week to lay the foundation for a trusting relationship.

First, consider actions that establish you more as a fellow learner than as a source of wisdom. It may be helpful to do things as *equal partners* in the early days of your relationship. For instance, you might team-teach a lesson rather than offering to observe your new teacher. You might spend time working in each other's classrooms, or you might take a trip to the media center to prepare classroom materials together. Many new teachers appreciate it when their partners invite them out to lunch or to a local happy hour to get away from the school setting.

Second, use your early conversations to analyze the new teacher's interpersonal style and willingness to accept help. Rowley (1999) states,

> The good mentor is effective in different interpersonal contexts. . . . Good mentor teachers recognize that each mentoring relationship occurs in a unique, interpersonal context. Beginning teachers can display widely different attitudes toward the help offered by a mentor. Just as good teachers adjust their teaching behaviors and communications to meet the needs of individual students, good mentors adjust their mentoring communications to meet the needs of individual mentees. (p. 21)

By listening attentively to your new teacher partner, you will be better able to adjust your own communication style. Good mentors are also flexible in the level and kind of support they provide, differentiating it to meet individual new teachers' changing needs. Early conversations can allow you to ascertain the areas in which your new teacher feels well prepared and those in which he or she will most likely need support in the near future. Listening to your partner talk about his or her work, concerns, and strengths can help you gently offer aid in ways that convey your faith in his or her ability to solve problems in a supportive atmosphere.

Helpful Help

- "I entered all the student information into the computer for her report cards."
- "I packed a snack and sat with him in his classroom each day after school to debrief."
- "I did library research for her as she planned a unit on Anne Frank."
- "I administered the reading assessment for her and helped her interpret the results."
- "We made a date for nightly e-mail conversation time."

In addition, you can begin to provide assistance that is most valued at the time by your new teacher partner, allowing him or her (to the extent possible) to set the agenda for your work together. We asked a group of support providers for their most notable recent successes in working with their new teachers. The examples in the textbox indicate that support providers offered assistance in a variety of arenas, all dictated by their partners. "Support" may not be "support" unless it is perceived as helpful by the beginning teacher. Support providers convey and build trust when they remain flexible, listen carefully, and gather evidence to determine the level and kind of support needed by the new teacher.

As you use the early days of your partnership to establish a collegial relationship, you increase the likelihood that your support will be appropriate, that your partner will value it, and that you will aid your new teacher in ways that drive your partner's practice forward. The early weeks of your partnership can also be used for building communication structures and strategies.

BUILDING COMMUNICATION STRUCTURES

Communication is so important that it is discussed in many of this book's chapters, with Chapter 3 devoted entirely to it. This section builds on the foundation presented in Chapter 3 by describing efforts you can pursue during the earliest days of the relationship to develop clear expectations, feedback mechanisms, and strategies for communicating with your new teacher partner.

Clear Expectations

Most of us function best when we understand the roles, rules, and conditions under which we work. Especially given the challenging conditions under which teachers work, it is important to make rules that are often tacit explicit. Some communication norms seem consistent across sites and professional settings. For example, new employees should listen more than they talk. Does that hold true at your site? If so, advise your partner to be quick to listen and slow to judge or express opinions, at least publicly. Other norms for communication may be specific to your site. By which name shall your partner call the custodian? The administrator? Is he or she allowed to make requests directly of the secretary? What is lounge talk like at your site? Do you have any recommendations for interacting successfully with other staff members?

> **Things *NOT* to Say to a Student Teacher During the First Week**
>
> - "I really didn't want a student teacher. They made me take one."
> - "I just found out today that I'm having a student teacher."
> - "My *last* student teacher was the greatest!"
> - "Why would you want to go into this business anyway?"
> - "You can assume you're doing just fine unless I tell you otherwise."
> - "..." (Nothing)
>
> Try developing alternatives to these statements. We will check with you at the end of the chapter.

Additionally, you will foster your partner's chances for success within the classroom if you develop guidelines for communication between the two of you. Do you want your partner to tell you if you make a content error, and vice versa? Will you provide feedback to each other in front of the students? When does each of you find is the best time to talk? When does each of you like to be left alone? Though it may feel awkward to launch a conversation about communication expectations, clear and shared expectations will pave the way for success throughout the term.

In addition to building the norms for clear communication early on, you will also help your partner if you specify up front, to the extent possible, your expectations regarding your classroom and his or her performance. Begin by thinking through the tacit rules by which you operate during your daily professional life to extract critical factors. Then decide how—and how much—you will share in the building of a set of shared expectations. Communicate those expectations in clear and humane language. Table 5.1 asks a number of questions that may be useful for cooperating teachers as they spur a gentle conversation about classroom expectations.

Feedback Mechanisms

Student teachers and new teacher partners want and need feedback . . . lots of it! During the first weeks of your partnership, you can:

Table 5.1 Building Shared Expectations With Student Teachers

Topic	Possible Questions for Discussion
Planning	• What do you expect in terms of lesson planning? • Do lesson plans need to be written out? In what format? How far in advance? • Do you expect long-term plans, kept in a plan book?
Curriculum and Instruction	• How closely must the student teacher follow the adopted texts? May he or she try things that are not in the texts? • What do you expect in terms of instructional strategies? Is cooperative learning okay? Do you want to see direct instruction? • Will you ever intervene during a lesson? Under what conditions? • Who grades what? Which papers will the student teacher be expected to grade?
Discipline and Management	• How much noise do you tolerate? • How much latitude does the student teacher have in changing the discipline plan? Moving the desks? • Do you expect the student teacher to speak with the parents to follow through on discipline issues?
Professional Responsibilities	• When do you need to see the student teacher before school? When is he or she allowed to leave? (Be clear on the difference between the requirement and what will work best for you as a team.) • What is the student teacher's responsibility for supervision of students during breaks, recesses, and before and after school? • Will the student teacher be photocopying? (Many student teachers feel like aids when they are asked to stand over the machine. If student teachers are expected to photocopy, have a rationale—and there is one!—well planned and ready for presentation.) • What will be the student teacher's responsibilities during parent conferences? Grading periods? • How, in general, are student teachers expected to contribute to the school?

- Establish the expectation that you *will* communicate regularly.
- Make a plan for how and when you will talk about teaching performance.
- Select communication strategies that will be most useful for you and your partner.

Take five minutes or so during the first few days you and your partner are together and share oral communication strategies that have proven helpful to each of you in the past, given your communication styles and individual personalities. Many partners like early morning or after-school conversations when the room is quiet and both partners can think without interruptions. Others prefer after-dinner telephone conversations. When and how will you communicate orally? Consider pulling out your plan book and setting out 10 minutes or so each day or 30 minutes per week for a meeting with your partner. In the coming weeks, examine your communication plan. If it is not working for both of you, change it.

You may also wish to arrange a "code" system for communicating with your student teacher during lessons. This system can allow you two to share information that you do not wish students to understand. Using coded verbal cues, gestures, or actions for circumstances such as the following can help your student teacher save face, maintain authority with the students, and still get your assistance when the need arises:

- The student teacher could relate, "Help! I'm losing control of these rebels!" by a prearranged signal, such as standing up and handing the cooperating teacher a piece of paper.
- The cooperating teacher could nonverbally say, "Take a look at Pat, who is eating a glue stick in the back of the room" by nodding in Pat's direction and tapping a finger on his or her lips.
- The cooperating teacher could tacitly ask, "This lesson could use a little team teaching; mind if I join in?" by inquiring, "Mr. Ortiz, I had an interesting experience with this; may I share it now?"

Establishing the code now, before you need to use it, can set the expectation that it is natural to need support and that your job is to provide thoughtful, sometimes discrete assistance as your student teacher learns to teach.

Written communication is also essential. Written communication provides important documentation that may be required by the university or induction program, culminating in the summative evaluation you write at the term's end. Sitting down and discussing the final evaluation now can help you select written feedback strategies that you and your partner value and that provide ongoing information related to the evaluation's categories. Additionally, an effective mentor differentiates his or her support to match the needs of the mentee, and a conversation about the evaluation's categories, format, and standards can provide the target for your work together by clarifying the student teacher's self-perceived areas of strength and areas needing support.

Written feedback can also encourage reflection by capturing experiences and emotions and freezing them so that they can be examined later, after the press of the lesson and school day pass. Many partners like using dialogue journals because journals do not require real-time, face-to-face interaction. Consider locating a composition book that can be used for written conversations and brief notes. Some

Table 5.2 A Student Teacher's Weekly Report Card

My Goals for This Week	My Grade Performance	My Cooperating Teacher's Grade of My Performance	My Supervisor's Grade of My Performance
I wait until I have the students' attention before I begin a lesson.	A	A	B
I follow through on discipline statements and requests once I make them.	C	B+	B
I include at least one active participation strategy per	A–	A+	A+

partners find e-mail a productive way to facilitate conversation, so exchange e-mail addresses if that works best for the two of you. Ensure that you have a thick stack of lesson observation forms from the university. Make a plan to use one or two, starting right away.

Your partner may also have thoughts on the feedback mechanisms he or she hopes you will include. We know one student teacher, for instance, who was inspired by "literary report cards" (Yopp & Yopp, 1992). She translated the strategy into a weekly report card for herself (see Table 5.2) that was highly effective feedback mechanism for several reasons: (1) she initiated it herself, (2) her cooperating teacher was trusting and flexible enough to let her try it, and (3) it provided a great starting point for conversations among the supervisor–student teacher–cooperating teacher triad. Early discussions of verbal and written feedback strategies can help you and your partner establish habits of communicating and select feedback strategies that are effective for both of you.

PLANNING THE STUDENT TEACHING EXPERIENCE

"By failing to prepare, you are preparing to fail."

—Benjamin Franklin
(quoted in Creative Quotations, 2002)

One way you can slow down your spinning merry-go-round classroom so that your new teacher partner can hop safely aboard is to take an hour to plan the student teaching experience. Making a plan will alleviate anxiety, help the student teacher take control of his or her obligations and growth, and ensure that your time is carefully directed toward efforts that will meet the end goal.

Our research (Guillaume & Rudney, 1993, 2002) shows us that many student teachers want *freedom*. Freedom, in the eyes of student teachers, means having the opportunity to plan their own lessons, to use their own developing discipline strategies, to spend time with the students as the person in charge, and to make mistakes. However, student teachers also tell us that freedom needs to be carefully structured so that student teachers have the support of their cooperating teachers as colleagues who will step in if they flounder. The textbox gives student teachers' quotes related to the cooperating teacher's delicate balancing act of providing freedom with support.

What Student Teachers Say About Freedom

- "My [cooperating teacher] gave me the opportunity to take things over at my pace. She did not rush me into anything that I was not ready for. . . . She let me experience some of my own things while still guiding and supporting me."

- "The most helpful thing she did was let me teach. She allowed me freedom to come up with my own ideas. She encouraged me to try out things that I learned from workshops. She stepped back and let me correct my own mistakes, all the while guiding me with little hints and suggestions."

- "[She] gave me my independence. She offered support, but always allowed me the opportunity to learn from my mistakes."

- "[She] gave me an increasing amount of freedom that was enough to establish myself but still the right amount to succeed."

You can support your student teacher's drive for independence by devising a plan for his or her assumption of responsibility: When will you observe each other? Which subject areas or times of the day will the student teacher take over first? Later? In the plan, outline teaching responsibilities, special lessons, and week(s) when the student teacher is to be in charge. Exercise 5.2 lays out a guideline for a five-week student teaching experience that may give you some ideas about structuring a similar plan for your own situation.

Several sources of information can help you devise the assumption of responsibility plan. You have already spent some time getting to know your student teacher and discussing his or her prior experiences. The assumption of responsibility plan should reflect your student teacher's strengths and skills. Does the university expect different kinds of experiences from the student teacher? If there are competencies to be met, your responsibilities plan can include things that might require extra effort to bring about (e.g., using certain kinds of technology or working with students who have specific needs).

Read over any printed information from the university regarding requirements for your student teacher and make note of the questions you have for the university supervisor. Your student teacher can also share with you major instructional emphases from his or her course work. Your district's mandates and your own long-term plans will also figure into the assumption of responsibility plan. This plan will probably change over time, but writing it early typically puts student teachers at ease and helps both partners work toward common purposes.

BECOMING FAMILIAR WITH THE STUDENTS, CLASSROOM, SCHOOL, AND LOCAL CONTEXT

Student teachers and new teachers alike will need assistance in understanding the local context that shapes their work. Knowledge of the students, classroom, school, district, and neighborhood will help your partner effectively meet the needs of the learners and perform other duties of teaching well.

Getting to Know the Students

Though teachers differ in their views of the information they view as relevant, your new teacher may benefit from studying information about students' developmental progress, their cultural capital (the rich traditions and knowledge they bring to the classroom from home), their interests and preferences, their current level of performance, and the services they receive. Box 5.2 provides some strategies that your new teacher may use to get to know students. Together, select a few (or suggest your own) that will help your partner gather information that will assist him or her in helping the students learn.

Getting to Know the Classroom

Many student teachers, especially those with some classroom experience, worry about fitting in to an experienced teacher's classroom (Guillaume & Rudney, 1993). Desks are already arranged, bulletin boards are posted, curriculum is planned. You can capitalize on (or build) the student teacher's desire to fit into your classroom by sharing information about life in your room. The student teacher will benefit both from lofty information, such as your educational philosophy and approaches to learning and discipline, as well as from routine procedural information that keeps your classroom functioning. If you have a mission statement, share it. If there are favorite quotations that guide you as an educator, talk about those. Some of the work you did in the "Getting to Know Each Other as Professionals" exercises you tried in Chapter 3 may be helpful.

The more student teachers know about the classroom structure and routine procedures, the better they can focus their teaching efforts. Exercise 5.3 presents a note-taking guide for issues of procedures and routines. There are many ways to gather and share information on procedures. Some cooperating teachers place this information in a three-ring binder that they present to the student teacher on the first day. Others may provide a blank note-taking guide and allow the student teacher to record, through observing the first days, as much information as possible. This focuses early observations and provides a starting point for a conversation about the classroom. Others hold a "walk through" during the early days of the placement to point out relevant supplies and materials.

As you discuss classroom procedures, you may wish to address the latitude that the student teacher has to make changes in those procedures. On the one hand, the student teacher is present to learn from your experience and should not disrupt learning for the students. On the other hand, no two teachers are the same, and

---

Box 5.2 Suggesting Strategies for Getting to Know Students

☐ *Attitude surveys and general questionnaires:* The new teacher can borrow from published sources or develop others. Responses can be multiple choice, written, or drawn.

☐ *Observational data:* The new teacher can observe the students during instruction and during break times (e.g., recess at the elementary level), taking informal notes about their interactions, energy levels, and social patterns.

☐ *Student Interviews:* The new teacher can interview students in small groups or individually by having lunch with them or by pulling a few aside for small group conversations.

☐ *Expert Interviews:* The new teacher can talk with parents or site personnel who hold specialized knowledge about the students, including aspects such as their cultural heritage, their background knowledge, and their needs.

☐ *Charts:* The new teacher can make a chart using a class list and record information about languages used at school and home, special services received by each student, or other pertinent topics.

☐ *Historical data:* The new teacher can examine the students' past work via such historical data as student portfolios, past report cards, your grade book, and cumulative records. (Check protocol to ensure that your partner is allowed access to this information.)

---

cooperating teachers' classrooms serve partly as laboratories for student teachers as they make their own mistakes, learn from them, and develop their own style.

Getting to Know the School and District

Your new teacher partner will also need help navigating the school site and the district. By providing information about the physical plant, stated policies and procedures, and unstated values and norms, you assist your partner in developing professional competence that extends beyond the classroom. Box 5.3 summarizes the information presented in this section as checkpoints for later reference.

Administrators, other teachers, parents, and staff at the school tend to be highly aware of student teachers and new teachers. Your partner may benefit from at least five kinds of information.

First, it may be helpful for you to discuss the district's and site's stated mission and to help uncover some of its values. For example, does your school value teacher collaboration, or is it a viewed as a sign of strength to work independently? Is there an unwritten norm for teachers to participate heavily in after-school events and clubs? Knowledge of such values might help your new teacher partner avoid misstepping. Second, your partner needs to understand professional expectations. Provide information such as

---

Box 5.3 Checkpoints for Navigating the School Site and District Site

---

School and District Expectations
- ☐ Site and district mission and values
- ☐ Professional expectations (dress code, workday, supervision duty)
- ☐ School procedures (emergencies, sick students, library use, classroom visitors, reporting suspected abuse, calling in sick, substitute teacher procedures)

Physical Resources
- ☐ Physical plant (map and tour of school, district as appropriate)
- ☐ Supplies and materials (ordering materials and equipment, duplicating and laminating)

Personnel Resources
- ☐ Teachers
- ☐ Specialists and paraprofessionals
- ☐ Parents and other volunteers

- Dress code
- Teacher workday (hours)
- Supervision duty

Third, your partner will find information related to schoolwide procedures helpful. What are the policies regarding

- Emergencies (including disasters)?
- Sick students?
- Use of the library or media center?
- Classroom visitors?

- Calling in sick?
- Substitute teacher procedures?
- Procedures for reporting suspected child abuse?

Fourth, novices can better encourage student learning armed with good understanding of the physical plant and the resources available to them. Provide your partner with a map of the site and take him or her on a tour. Point out labs, the media center, and other special facilities that can serve your students. It may be appropriate to ask your partner to visit other carefully chosen and forewarned teachers to examine their different approaches and classroom layouts. Take a trip to the district office, if appropriate, examining the curricular materials and instructional services available there. Explain procedures for obtaining materials from the school or district. Such procedures may include

- Ordering audiovisual materials and equipment
- Obtaining specialized materials such as paint or clay
- Making requests of the secretaries and custodians
- Checking out software and hardware for computer-assisted instruction
- Duplicating, laminating, and preparing transparencies

Information regarding these policies and procedures may be available in district and school site handbooks. If so, make handbooks available to your partner, perhaps suggesting that he or she place them in a notebook after looking them over.

Fifth, you can help build your new partner's ideas about differentiated instruction and professional collaboration by helping him or her become aware of the personnel who serve as resources for students—paraprofessionals and specialists such as psychologists, speech and language therapists, special educators, social workers, police, and parents who are part of the educational program at your school or district. Many new teachers need help utilizing parent volunteers, senior citizens, and observers effectively. Discuss your program for incorporating volunteers, or introduce your partner to a fellow teacher who has a particularly strong system. Discuss the referral processes for students with special needs, and invite your partner to a meeting with other professionals, such as a Student Study Team or an Early Intervention meeting, related to serving students as a wider community of professionals. Each of these actions can help the new teacher to gain a sense of the many personnel resources who can work together to provide for an education that meets the varying needs of students.

Getting to Know the Neighborhood

Schools sometimes operate in isolation of the neighborhoods and communities they serve (Moll, Amanti, Neff, & Gonzalez, 1992). Rather than acknowledging and drawing upon the expertise, traditions, and values of local families, schools often ignore the knowledge found in surrounding neighborhoods. Fortunately, many schools do effectively address family needs, with most effective parent involvement programs sharing components such as a commitment to involve low-income parents, family empowerment as a major goal, and strong commitment to build on the values, structures, languages, and cultures of the home (Nieto, 1996). One approach (Gonzalez, Andrade, Civil, & Moll, 2001; Moll et al., 1992) is to draw upon the "funds of knowledge" that exist in every family and community. In their study of Latino communities in Arizona, Moll and his colleagues found that families have social networks wherein their extensive knowledge of construction, mining, sewing, and other topics is shared. By viewing parents and community members as rich and valuable resources, schools can build links to the community and provide educational experiences that are centered in meaning and linked to the life of the community.

Invite your new teacher partner to get acquainted with the local neighborhoods. A walking or driving tour of the neighborhoods can provide a first introduction. Teachers can also engage in research by speaking with students, families, and local businesspeople to gain a richer sense of the resources that the community brings to the school. Student projects, such as oral history interviews and parent visits to the classroom, can also provide information. It is important that, as your partner seeks information from parents, you help him or her remain sensitive to the different communication norms families may have (Davidman & Davidman, 1997). For instance, in many cultures a question such as, "How do you discipline your child at home?" might be considered impolite and outside the scope of a teacher's responsibility. Though it will require tact and sensitivity, your partner's effort to view families and the community as a resource and to gather information from these sources can enhance students' schooling experiences dramatically.

PARTING WORDS

This chapter laid out a great deal of work to be done during the first week of a new teacher partnership. This underscores the fact that there is much to know to succeed as a classroom teacher . . . without even viewing the instructional functions of the profession! There is indeed much to accomplish as a supporter of a new professional. Take another day if you need it.

P.S.: We said we'd check back. Did you develop alternatives for things NOT to say to a student teacher the first week? Compare yours with ours.

Instead of . . .	Try . . .
• "I really didn't want a student teacher. They made me take one."	• "I'm glad you're here!"
• "I just found out today that I'm having a student teacher."	• "I'm glad you're here! Here's a place for your things."
• "My *last* student teacher was the greatest!"	• "I learn so much from student teachers!"
• "Why would you want to go into this business anyway?"	• "You've made a demanding career choice! What brings you here?"
• "You can assume you're doing just fine unless I tell you otherwise."	• "You and I will talk regularly about how things are going."
• ". . ." (Nothing)	• "I'm glad you're here!"

EXERCISES

Exercise 5.1 First Week: The Off-and-Running Report Card

You may wish to use this summary of the chapter's points as a planing guide, a checksheet, or a reflective prompt.

Activity	Notes	√
Using the First Week to Build Your Relationship		
1. Create a physical space for student teacher.		
2. Consider a welcome token.		
3. Share information on student teacher's strengths and interests with students and families.		
4. Spend time talking and working together as colleagues.		
5. Discuss roles and responsibilities of each partner.		
6. Establish habits of active listening.		
Building Communication Structures		
1. Discuss the norms for communication at your site.		
2. Establish the boundaries of your communication with each other.		
3. Discuss expectations for classroom performance.		
4. Select oral feedback strategies.		
5. Select written feedback strategies		

Exercise 5.1 Continued

Activity	Notes	√
6. Develop coded language.		
7. Review the summative evaluation form.		
Planning the Student Teaching Experience		
1. Review the university's expectations.		
2. Examine other data (e.g., curriculum standards).		
3. Write an assumption of responsibility plan.		
Becoming Familiar With the Students, Classroom, School, and Local Context		
1. Help the new teacher gather information about the students.		
2. Share information about your classroom procedures, structures, and activities.		
3. Tour the school and discuss policies, procedures, and expectations.		
4. Get to know the community and its families.		

Exercise 5.2 Assumption of Responsibility Plan

Use this chart, or make one to match your circumstances, to plan the student teacher's assumption of classroom responsibilities. Try our codes or insert your own notes.

Code: ct = cooperating teacher; st = student teacher; o = observe; tt = team teach; t = solo teach

Subject Area/ Time of Day	Week 1	Week 2	Week 3	Week 4	Week 5
Opening					
Reading/ Language Arts					
Read Aloud					
Math					

Exercise 5.2 Continued

Science					
Social Studies					
Physical Education					
The Arts					
Other					

Exercise 5.2 Continued

Secondary School Example

Codes: ct = cooperating teacher; st = student teacher; o = observe; tt = team teach; t = solo teach

Period/Subject	Week 1	Week 2	Week 3	Week 4	Week 5
1:					
2:					
3:					
4:					
5:					
6:					
7:					

Exercise 5.3 Getting to Know Our Classroom

Use this form to take some notes before describing your classroom to your partner. Or, allow your student teacher to take the notes during observation periods or while you talk.

Some Questions	Our Room's Answers to Those Questions
Discipline Plan 1. What is the discipline plan? 2. What are the classroom rules? How are they determined? 3. What (if any) are the positive and negative consequences for student behaviors? 4. What role do the families play in the discipline plan? 5. Does the plan involve other teachers (e.g., for timeouts)? 6. Are there legal or local issues that influence how students are disciplined?	
Scheduling 1. What is the daily and weekly schedule? 2. Is there teaming with teachers in other rooms? If so, when and how? 3. Will other students be joining the room at any time? 4. Is there a schedule of when students leave for special services?	
Seating Arrangements 1. Where do students sit? 2. How are seats selected? 3. How often do they change?	
Attendance Procedures 1. When is attendance taken each day? 2. What form is used?	

Exercise 5.3   Continued

Some Questions	*Our Room's Answers to Those Questions*
3. How is information collected, and how does it get to the office? 4. What happens if a student enters tardy or leaves early?	
Homework 1. What is the policy for what kind, how much, and when homework is given? 2. Where are assignments recorded? 3. How and when is homework completion recorded? 4. Who checks it? How? Are homework grades recorded? 5. What are the consequences if students do not complete assignments?	
Classroom Procedures 1. When (if ever) are students allowed to sharpen pencils? 2. What happens if a student forgets classroom materials? 3. Where are classroom supplies stored? 4. What rules govern the use of supplies? 5. How are materials distributed and collected?	
Bathroom Procedures 1. When are students allowed to use the bathroom? 2. What if they need to go during a nonallowed time? 3. How many may leave at once?	

6

Helping Novices Learn the Roles of Teaching

"My cooperating teacher makes it look so easy." "The time you spend with the students is such a small part of the day." "People have no idea how much goes into teaching!"

—Student teachers after their first few weeks in the classroom

"I could drown in the paperwork. No one told me!" "I thought student *teaching was difficult. Student teachers have no clue how difficult* teaching *will be!"*

—New teachers

These opening quotations may reflect ubiquitous visions of how teaching will be. When we choose teaching as a profession—at 4 or at 40—many of us conjure up images of ourselves standing in front of a class or kneeling beside a student, our voices calm and low, our bearing benevolent. We look into eager faces and witness the glow of new

> "Housework is a breeze. Cooking is a pleasant diversion. Putting up a retaining wall is a lark. But teaching is like climbing a mountain."
>
> —Fawn M. Brodie
> (quoted in Creative Quotations, 2002)

learning we have kindled. Only with experience do we discover that the role of a teacher is more complicated and multifaceted, that the job of teaching involves many kinds of demands and numerous conflicting directives.

This chapter explores the complexity of teaching and suggests strategies that may aid you as you work with your new teacher partner to build competence in the many facets of teaching. Sections address the following topics:

- The complexity of teaching
- The layeredness of the experienced teacher partner's role
- Supporting competence in a multifaceted profession

THE COMPLEXITY OF TEACHING

Nearly 40 years of research document the complexity of classroom teaching, and life does not appear to be becoming any simpler for teachers today. Teaching is a demanding profession because teachers face complex conditions, fill many roles, hold differing visions of their work, manage tensions, and uphold moral obligations as well.

Complex Conditions

The physical, social, and time-bound characteristics of classrooms make them complex. Classrooms are crowded, public places where power is unequally distributed (Jackson, 1968). They are multidimensional places where many people with different desires and talents engage in scores of tasks and activities, vying for limited supplies to accomplish an array of personal and social objectives (Doyle, 1986). All of these people with their different goals engaging in rapidly paced and simultaneous activities make classrooms inherently unpredictable. Many things happen—and they happen at the same time!—so that teachers must act with very little time to think first. In Wasserman's (1999) words, "Being a teacher means accepting that things never go as we think they will. It means being prepared for the inevitability of the unexpected" (p. 468).

Because classrooms are so unpredictable, teaching has many effects, and those effects are difficult to know. First, our effects as teachers can be far-reaching and initially unseen (Jackson, 1986). Do *your* teachers, for instance, know of the effect they had on *you?* Additionally, results can vary for different students, so a single action can have dissimilar results depending on the unique characteristics of the student and his or her relationship with the teacher. Further, one decision can have multiple consequences. The things we do to bring about a particular result can have outcomes—some unintended—in other domains as well. For example, a teacher needs to have a calm environment that is conducive to learning, so the teacher may publicly sanction students' behaviors to encourage their attention to the lesson: "I like the way Emily and Cherise are sitting so nicely! Thank you!" What are possible intended and unintended effects of this well-meaning statement? On Emily and Cherise? On the boys in the classroom? On students of a different race than Emily and Cherise? On others?

Classrooms are also complex because they are shaped by time and by their surroundings. Each day's proceedings and world happenings contribute to tomorrow's norms and events in every classroom. Additionally, classrooms are molded by the many physical, social, political, and organizational settings that surround them. For instance, Goodlad (1990) points to myriad school-level factors that influence classrooms and the teachers within them. A sampling includes grouping and tracking policies and practices, recess and lunch schedules, and practices for selecting and distributing instructional materials. Further, the district, community—including parents—and larger political influences (e.g., state and federal legislation) affect life in classrooms as well. A recent example is the increased attention to student achievement as measured by standardized tests.

Teachers' Many Roles

Because of the complex conditions they face, teachers are required to serve many roles. Jackson (1968) mentions the supply sergeant and timekeeper roles that result from the crowded and hurried conditions of classroom life. Other roles, generated by preservice teachers, are listed in the textbox. No doubt you can add more. To complicate matters, some of the roles that teachers are expected to serve can actually conflict. For instance, how can a teacher serve as a student's advocate one

Some Roles of the Teacher
√ instructor
√ manager
√ entertainer
√ assessor
√ counselor
√ advocate
√ jailer
√ director

moment and as his or her judge the next? A similar tension may be found between the encouraging role a teacher serves one day and the gatekeeping role he or she assumes the next, a role that may bar a student from certain programs or services. Teachers must be many things to many people all the time. Additionally, they have their own views of the work they do.

Teachers' Visions of Their Work

Teachers enter the profession with orientations toward their work and answers (we hope) to questions such as "What does it mean to teach well?" These answers are formed based on their years as students, their life experiences, and their serious (we hope) consideration of the visions they want to realize as educators. Chapter 2 addresses some of the ways in which new teachers' thinking may differ and develop over time. Understanding teachers' visions of their work can serve to illuminate the dilemmas they face.

Though many differences in teacher ideology exist, one notable contrast is the contrast between a teacher's self-perception as an implementer or as an innovator in his or her role as curricular planner and instructional leader. In a study of first- and second-year teachers, Rudney and Lea (2000) found teachers' disposition toward curriculum to be a powerful theme in understanding teacher decisions and actions. Teachers who might be characterized as implementers rely on existing curriculum and focus their efforts on adapting it to meet the needs of their students. Innovators focus instead on the creation of new materials. They prefer using their own ideas and often resist using a mandated curriculum. The disposition toward curriculum does not signal good or bad teachers; instead, it can help mentors and others understand a teacher's needs and expectations. For instance, implementers may benefit from clear expectations and modeling. They may be excellent members on curriculum review committees because of their interest in and knowledge of program features. Innovators may benefit from general rather than specific guidelines and may feel their best when allowed to brainstorm and create. The mandated use of certain curricula would necessarily present very different problems for teachers with these contrasting orientations.

Tensions in Teaching

Teachers' orientations, the need to fill contrasting roles, and the immensely complex conditions of the classroom can all produce a set of dilemmas and intractable tensions that teachers must manage daily. Historically, some tensions in American schooling include the simultaneous struggles for equity and excellence, for student autonomy in the face of teacher authority, and for care and control concurrently exhibited by the teacher. One recent example of a tension teachers manage is centered on standards-based curricula. Some teachers struggle with maintaining their "start with the student" ideology and realizing the potential of high expectations for all of America's children.

Decision making in teaching, then, is often not a straightforward or simple process. As Lampert (1985) illustrates, even so seemingly clear cut a decision as "What should this student learn?" is fraught with implications and weighty consequences for the teacher:

> My aims for any one particular student are tangled with my aims for each of the others in the class, and more importantly, I am responsible for choosing a course of action in circumstances where choice leads to further conflict. The contradictions between goals I am expected to accomplish thus become continuing inner struggle about how to do my job. (p. 182)

Dilemmas and tensions in teaching may not to be apparent to us when—at 4 or 40—we envision ourselves spreading the light of wisdom over an eager audience, but they await us each day as we make the difficult decisions that are an inexorable part of what it means to be an educator.

The Moral Dimension of Teaching

Managing dilemmas and tensions requires teachers to venture into domains of teaching that may not be readily apparent to the novice. For many teachers, that first distant image of "self as teacher" may focus on student learning, or on positive social relations, or on the technical skills of teaching. What is most likely missing from that distant image is a clear focus on the moral dimension of teaching.

> "Our whole life is startlingly moral. There is never an instant's truce between virtue and vice."
>
> —Henry David Thoreau
> (quoted in Creative Quotations, 2002)

"Morals" and "ethics" are the rules of conduct that govern how people should act and how they should treat each other. Because teaching is a human action undertaken in regard to other humans, it is fundamentally a moral enterprise (Fenstermacher, 1990). Whenever a question involves what is fair, right, or just, it is a moral question. So, according to Fenstermacher, whenever a teacher requires students to share (or not share), whenever a teacher decides who should go first (and not first), and whenever a teacher intervenes in a schoolground argument, he or she is acting as a moral agent. A teacher cannot even speak with his or her students during a lesson without exercising authority in a situation of unequal power, thereby acting in the moral dimension (Buzzelli & Johnston, 2001).

Many of the moral dilemmas teachers may face in the classroom, according to Kidder and Born (1998–1999), will be of the "right versus right" variety, wherein there

---

Box 6.1   Four Kinds of Moral Dilemmas

1—Truth versus loyalty
   (One's personal honesty or integrity is at odds with one's responsibility and promise keeping)

2—Short term versus long term
   (Requirements of the present are at odds with foresight, stewardship, or deferred gratification)

3—Justice versus mercy
   (Fairness and the expectation of equal application of the rules is at odds with empathy or compassion)

4—Individual versus community
   (What is best for the individual is at odds with what is best for the community)

SOURCE: Drawn from Kidder & Born (1998–1999)

---

is a conflict between courses of action that are both in some sense right. For instance, should a child who frequently disrupts cooperative group lessons be removed from the group? He or she needs the opportunity to learn and practice social skills, and the child's peers need the opportunity to focus on their work. This is a dilemma of the individual versus the community, which, along with three other dilemmas, is presented in Box 6.1.

Further, a teacher's moral charge goes far beyond his or her individual decisions about what to say and how to behave with students. The entire process of schooling is a moral responsibility (Goodlad, 1990) because schools' primary functions, those of enculturating the

> "The test of the morality of a society is what it does for its children."
>
> —Dietrich Bonhoeffer
> (quoted in Creative Quotations, 2002)

young and providing access to knowledge for all, are moral callings. These callings require the professional community to deliberate just and proper courses of action. Additionally, teachers accept membership in a profession, they accept its code of ethics (Soltis, 1986). They are no longer individuals acting solely under their own accord. They accept the moral obligation to their clients, including promises such as the commitment to help people learn, to represent the subject matter honestly and fairly, and to protect the students entrusted to them.

Thus, though teachers may profess not to teach values and may rush through days guided by "to do" lists, they cannot escape the moral weight of their work. Each of a teacher's actions as an individual, as an employee, and as a member of the profession of education can be seen in terms of its moral implications. In the face of complex and morally laden conditions, teachers accept the burden of making decisions about what is right and what is best for our children.

THE LAYEREDNESS OF THE EXPERIENCED TEACHER PARTNER'S ROLE

We hope we have fueled your renewed respect for the powerful and difficult work you do as a classroom teacher. Now upon that recognition can be layered the potential impact you have on learners, teachers, and the profession in your work as a mentor.

Just as classroom teaching requires making decisions under complex and challenging conditions, your work as a mentor is a multifaceted and demanding affair. As a cooperating teacher, you must make decisions under the scrutiny of an adult who draws inferences about teaching based on your example filtered through his own perspective and whose very presence changes the nature of your classroom. Also, you have accepted the responsibility to help another person join the profession of education, with its many tensions and nuances, while simultaneously managing its many roles and demands.

Helping a new professional learn to teach requires you to expend efforts that go far beyond classroom teaching responsibilities. Mentorship is based upon a healthy relationship among the partners and the faculty or leadership team members of the induction program, and the ongoing communication among the parties is plain hard work. Mentorship also requires skills in fostering adult learning and includes providing tactful, accurate, and systematic feedback. This feedback and support entails that you understand characteristics of adult learners and the trajectory of teacher development in general and then apply your knowledge to a specific new teacher partner. To provide appropriate feedback and support, you are required to carefully analyze you partner's entry-level experiences, strengths, and preferences.

Your multifaceted role as mentor also requires you to adjust the support you provide based on continuous analysis of your new teacher partner's needs. As circumstances change, so must the support you provide. At times, support may be directive, collaborative, or nondirective, as illustrated in Table 6.1. In selecting the level of intervention appropriate for a particular instance, you can take what you know about your partner's current expertise, style, developmental level and state of mind and compare it with the immediacy of the situation. Situations in which your students or partner are in physical, emotional, or legal danger may well require swift, directive support from you. Many other situations may be best addressed with limited, supportive intervention. Recall that student teachers generally prefer the highest degree of freedom that still allows for their success (Guillaume & Rudney, 2002).

Your role as mentor requires you to provide differentiated support not only for classroom issues, such as classroom management and instruction, but also for the other domains of professional behavior, such as acting effectively within the organization (see, for instance, Shepston & Jensen, 1997) and attending to the ethical requirements of the profession. How can you use your knowledge and skills in teaching and mentoring to support growth for teachers as they join our profession?

Table 6.1 Examples of Experienced Teacher Behaviors Within a Continuum of Support

Directive Support (Prescriptive or authoritative)	Collaborative Support (Facilitative)	Nondirective Support (Reflective)
• Set the agenda. • Identify issues and problems and communicate them to the new teacher. • Provide information and direct instruction. • Offer suggestions, advice, and assistance. • Suggest specific modifications. • Provide materials. • Evaluate new teacher performance without shared analysis.	• Guide new teacher toward setting a shared agenda. • Help new teacher focus on issues and problems by providing information for reflection. • Co-construct ideas to try, hypotheses to test. • Discuss ranges of options and materials. • Suggest resources. • Facilitate evaluation of new teacher performance through discussion of evidence and the new teacher's perspectives.	• Allow new teacher to set the agenda. • Use active listening as new teacher identifies issues and problems. • Model professional practice without cuing. • Foster new teacher's self analysis of issues, actively supporting new teacher's initiative. • Encourage new teacher's experimentation in the classroom. • Serve as a resource for new teacher, pointing him or her to other sources of information and expertise.

SOURCE: Inspired by the California Department of Education, 2002.

SUPPORTING COMPETENCE IN A MULTIFACETED PROFESSION

In helping your new teacher partner become a self-directed professional who displays competence across the many domains of teaching, five kinds of support may prove useful:

- Start with a vision
- Perceive and address classroom complexity
- Work across the range of teacher roles
- Honor the tensions of teaching
- Attend to the moral dimension of teaching

Start With a Vision

The new teachers' quotations at the beginning of this chapter serve as a reminder of how easy it can be for teachers to get swept up in the tide of immediate demands and other people's agendas. For new teachers especially, mere survival can quickly become equated with success. Goodlad (1990), however, reminds us that the complex conditions of the classroom require teacher judgment, and judgment involves the enactment of values. It is critical that teachers answer such important questions as "What are schools for?" to develop a sense of purpose for their work. Duffy (1998) similarly underscores the importance of creating a vision to guide one's daily actions under demanding conditions. Several of the most important contributions mentors, supervisors, and other teacher educators can make are to help new teachers clarify their professional visions, to sharpen those visions through their classroom practice, and to remain true to them as they manage the complexity of the classroom. Some of the following actions may assist your new teacher in envisioning and enacting a view of good practice:

- Describe your own vision of teaching, model it through your classroom and mentoring practices, and describe difficulties you experience in keeping it alive.
- Discuss your school site's vision, how it was developed, how it incorporates the views of the community, how it is enacted, and how it changes over time.
- Listen to your new teacher's vision, watch for it in classroom practice, and provide feedback about its enactment. Your partner may have written an educational philosophy as a course assignment. Exercise 6.1 can provide a starting point if your new teacher has not yet articulated his or her vision.
- Openly analyze conflicting visions and the dilemmas they present for both of you in your work.

Perceive and Address Classroom Complexity

"Teaching, real teaching, is—or ought to be—a messy business."

—Harry Crews
(quoted in Creative Quotations, 2002)

Many novices tend not to perceive the multiple dimensions of practice or the complicated conditions under which they work. The ability to perceive and address the complexity of teaching develops over time as new teachers become more skilled observers, but there are ways to help sharpen their perception:

Making meaning. Given the unpredictability of classrooms, teachers are required to *make meaning* during each minute of their day (Wasserman, 1999). To make meaning, teachers analyze situations, interpret them, and select actions based on their interpretations. Making meaning, according to Wasserman, is partly a personal affair because who we are and what we know as individuals shapes our interpretations. However, making meaning is also a process of collecting, analyzing, and acting upon classroom data in a way that can be fostered by a supportive partner. Mentors can help new teachers frame problems. By observing current events and comparing them to other situations, experienced teachers can then help their partners gather data, and they can help analyze data by extracting main ideas and generating hypotheses. Finally, they can aid their partner in selecting an action that is informed by earlier steps in the process. Mentors can also help their partners avoid traps in making meaning, such as acting upon untested assumptions, over-applying generalizations, viewing situations in terms of extremes, and treating personal bias as fact (Wasserman, 1999). Viewing new teacher partners' quest to learn to teach as one of *making meaning* rather than of *finding answers* can help them perceive classroom conditions in greater detail and can help them build practices that are more flexible and better integrated into a holistic understanding of teaching and all it entails.

Analyzing performance. New teacher partners may also become more perceptive and able to work under complex conditions if mentors help them analyze classroom performance—theirs and yours—in light of the full range of factors that influence classroom decision making. For instance, you might consider these strategies:

• When you model an instructional strategy or employ a practice, discuss the conditions under which the strategy is likely to be effective and factors that would limit its success. Discuss alternatives to that strategy and describe how you decide when to use which strategy.

• Ask your partner to observe you teach a lesson, then discuss it. In your discussion, note the various decision points you recall, the options you saw as viable, and the consequences you envisioned as you made your decisions. You can also talk about unintended consequences.

• Videotape a lesson (perhaps yours first, then one of your partner's) and view it together. Note the surprising elements that were not observed during the actual lesson. Try analyzing the lesson from a number of vantage points, such as lesson structure, the teacher's questioning behavior, or gender differences in teacher feedback. Pause the tape and discuss options at various decision points. Review written student feedback on the same lesson.

• During your post-lesson discussions, use probes that allow your partner to think about teaching in broader or deeper terms. Exercise 6.2 may be useful.

• When you offer advice or suggestions, be thoughtful about using a holistic or reductionist approach. In a holistic approach, you recognize the many factors that influence a performance and steer clear of discrete suggestions that may have limited applicability. In a reductionist approach, you pull apart a performance and address its component knowledge and skills. If you elect a reductionist approach, remember to place the pieces back into a coherent whole in your discussion and practice.

Work Across the Range of Teacher Roles

Based on your experience, what do new teachers struggle with most? They sometimes mention to us that the university did not prepare them to handle the paperwork burden. Or they comment that they do not know how to set up a grade book or refer a student for special services. Try making a list

> **Support Provider Note**
>
> New teachers often are very appreciative of assistance with their noninstructional duties.

of teacher roles that tend to be overlooked or underpracticed, in your view. A first step in helping your partner perceive the many roles of teaching might be to show him or her your list, modify it together, and determine immediate areas of concern. This activity might also help you succeed at the careful balancing act of providing just the right amount of exposure to and practice in the many roles of teaching. Too little exposure to the many roles of teaching may result in an ill-prepared teacher who struggles with the many demands placed upon him or her during the first year. Too much exposure and practice in the many roles can result in a resentful teacher who was unable to focus during student teaching on areas where he or she perceived the greatest need for growth.

As a cooperating teacher, it may help to:

• Ask your student teacher to shadow you throughout an entire day, making note of the many roles you serve and things you accomplish in addition to fostering student learning.

• Develop a plan for how and when you will introduce your student teacher to noninstructional duties. Begin with having a clear sense of the full range of these duties, perhaps by trying Exercise 6.3. As you plan, consider carefully the consequences of requiring certain duties or shielding your student teacher from the range of noninstructional duties.

• Provide direct instruction (including modeling and a chance to practice) as appropriate for some of your roles. For instance, you might share your principles and strategies for organizing and leading a parent conference, allow your student teacher to observe a few conferences, and then guide him or her in leading a conference.

• Additionally, you can help your partner address the full range of responsibilities of teaching by openly discussing your personal experiences and preferences. Do you hate serving as an assessor? Relish it? Which of your many roles seem to present dilemmas for you? Candid discussions such as these can help your partner see that filling multiple roles can be a challenge even for an experienced teacher, that ambivalence about some of these roles is not unusual, and that competence and job satisfaction do not hinge upon just one role.

Honor the Tensions of Teaching

Novices sometimes strive for certainty and for right answers, but your efforts to help your partner to realize his or her vision, to understand the richness of the classroom context, and to try on the many roles of teaching will almost certainly give rise to some of the tensions in teaching. We believe that you should talk openly with your partner about the conflicting demands and dilemmas you face. Frank conversations can teach your partner that:

• Wrestling with tensions is a part of the job; it does not mean things are going poorly.
• Dealing with dilemmas in sophisticated, thoughtful ways is an ethical responsibility.
• Competent professionals may struggle through the difficult decisions they face daily, may sail through some, may make mistakes in others, but nearly always survive them, learn from them, and move on to face the next set of challenges a bit wiser and a bit more sensitive to the dilemmas that await.

The textbox notes a few of the issues some cooperating teachers recently reported facing. Each of them had student teachers at the time and did an admirable job of showing their partners how they remained true to their own visions while still fulfilling their professional responsibilities to their sites and districts. How might you talk with a student teacher or newly credentialed teacher about each of these issues? What issues are you currently weighing? Do they include moral dimensions?

Attend to the Moral Dimension of Teaching

Your partner reports hearing that a nearby teacher wrote down items from the standardized test as students took it. What do you do as a teacher bound by the ethical code of your profession? Do you have further obligations as a mentor? What are they?

Mentors and others who work with new teachers have the responsibility of helping new teachers perceive, analyze, and deal with the ethical problems they may face (Howe, 1986). To meet this challenge we can enhance teachers' ethical consciousness or moral sensitivity, teach specific skills and strategies (Soltis, 1986), and serve as models of moral practice.

To heighten new teachers' sensitivity to the moral dimension of teaching, we can draw new teachers' attention to aspects of practice that exemplify the need for moral deliberation. These include questions of what is right and just. Examples include selecting consequences for infractions of classroom rules, plans for building cooperative groups, and decisions on how to distribute limited resources among class members. New teachers should come to see such questions as not purely technical ones but as ones that hold moral implications. New teachers should observe their mentors and colleagues engaging in moral deliberation—that is, demonstrating empathy for the perspectives of others, considering conflicting interests, and deliberating to select a course of action.

Mentors and other teacher educators can teach specific skills that enhance new teachers' ability to address moral dilemmas. These skills include, among others, interpersonal skills and reasoning skills. What about the standardized test example, given above? What about Kidder and Born's (1998–1999) earlier example of the student who disrupts cooperative learning lessons? Allowing such a student to participate provides him or her with the opportunity to gain social skills. Removing the student allows his or her peers to focus on the content. What should the teacher do?

A tool that mentors and other teacher educators can model and teach to new teachers involves analyzing moral dilemmas in three ways, thus adopting a language of ethical decision making that can be broadly applied. The textbox gives three ways of deliberating courses of action (Kidder & Born, 1998–1999). If teachers engage in *ends-based thinking*, they consider the potential result of each decision to choose a course of action. If teachers engage in *needs-based thinking*, they weigh the various parties' needs rather than potential results in making their decision. If, instead, teachers use *care-based thinking*, they operate out of a base of empathy and use "the golden rule" thinking to make a decision. By using the language of ethical deliberation, by modeling ethical practice, and by helping new teachers reason through classroom dilemmas, experienced teacher partners can support the growing competence of their new teacher partners across the moral dimension of teaching.

Some Recently Experienced Professional Discrepancies

- "My district has us focusing only on language arts and mathematics until test scores improve. This runs contrary to my philosophy of a curriculum drawing from the richness of the whole of the human experience."
- "We give standardized tests to our second graders. That is inconsistent with my view of child development."
- "We pull our English learners out for language assessment during their very first week. I think they need more time to acclimate to a new setting."

Three Ways to Think Through Dilemmas

1—ends-based thinking
2—needs-based thinking
3—care-based thinking

Our hope is that this chapter painted a realistic portrait of the classroom and provided some suggestions that can help you support your partner's practice across the many domains of teaching.

EXERCISES

Exercise 6.1   Articulating a Vision of Education

Invite your new teacher partner to write a brief vision or mission statement to capture his or her core convictions concerning education. Joining him or her in this endeavor can provide a useful point of comparison. Short statements can serve as powerful distillations of full philosophies. Try revising the statement until it fits on an index card that gets clipped on the plan book. Some of these questions may spark your thinking:

1. Think big. If you could accomplish just five things with students in a year, what would they be? Four things? Three things? Two? One?

2. What do good teachers do?

3. How do you know you are successful at the end of the day?

4. What would you like students to say about your influence on them if they were interviewed 10 years from now?

5. Try titling the mission statement "This I Believe" and writing just a few core convictions.

Exercise 6.2   Looking for Classroom Complexity

Try these techniques for exploring teaching.

1. *Student responses to instruction:* Choose target students with varying characteristics. What are their reactions to the lesson? (Examine student work, if available, or consider interviewing students.)

2. *The implicit curriculum:* What might students have learned about dimensions of the implicit—or hidden—curriculum through your lesson (e.g., how to behave, how to be a girl or boy, who has power)? How could you test your hypotheses by gathering information from students?

3. *Considering alternatives:* Choose a critical incident. What might have happened if . . . ? How might another teacher have handled it? What might have been the results of that?

4. *Your vision of teaching:* What do you believe is important about education? How/which parts of this lesson might work toward or against this vision?

Exercise 6.3 A Few of the Many Roles of Teaching

Select from among these choices to help your partner gain a sense of some of the roles of teaching.

1. *Manager of noninstructional duties:* Just for one day, make a list of all things you do related to the job (e.g., committee work, association work, parent contacts, managing paperwork requests from administration, photocopying, assessing student work, pursuing professional development, managing paraprofessionals, advocating for students for social services, attending meetings). Share your list with a colleague. What would he or she add? Then share it with your new teacher partner. Ask your partner to circle the ones he or she would like to learn about first.

2. *Subject matter expert:* Rank subjects you teach in order according to your perceptions of your expertise. Ask your partner to do the same. How do you learn the subject matter? How do you keep abreast of the content you are expected to teach when curricula, students, and times change?

3. *Classroom manager:* If classroom management involves running the business end of a classroom, how would you describe your work? Share a copy of your management plan. Send your partner around the school to observe some other management plans and talk with the teachers (if possible) about their decisions as managers.

4. *Disciplinarian:* How do you help students make responsible choices about their behavior? How do you prevent and correct misbehavior and encourage self-control and pro-social behavior? Share your classroom discipline plan.

5. *Instructional leader:* How do you teach? Why do you use that style or those approaches?

6. *Assessor:* What is your approach to assessing students' growth and learning? How do you manage a grade book? What are the forms of assessment you utilize? What have you seen other teachers use successfully? What are your worries about assessing and grading students' progress?

7. *Putting it together:* Take any two (or three) of the above roles and explain how they connect.

Exercise 6.4 Responding to a Case With Moral Implications

Read this case with your partner. Independently answer the questions that follow and then compare and discuss.

After struggling with whether he should give a "most improved" award to a student in his history class, Mr. Brown, a teacher at the local junior high school, decided to give the award. At the awards assembly, Mr. Brown announced that the student had a D- average at midterm but that by the end of the grading period he had raised his grade to a B. Mr. Brown invited the student on stage, warmly shook his hand, and gave him the "most improved" pin.

1. What, if any, ethical issues are involved in this case?

2. What are two "rights" that are at odds with each other in this case?

3. How might each of Kidder and Born's (1998–1999) kinds of ethical reasoning be used to approach this dilemma?

   • ends-based thinking

   • needs-based thinking

   • care-based thinking

4. Would you have given the award? If not, what would you have done?

7

Observation
and Feedback

"I taught my inquiry lesson today. My cooperating teacher graded papers during the lesson and never said a word to me when it was over. He hates me."

—A student teacher

Many novice teachers draw inaccurate conclusions based on the feedback— or lack thereof—they receive from mentors. Like the student teacher who made the comment above, *your* mentee cares about what you think and needs to hear from you. Building on positive communication already established, you will need to formulate and communicate specific information about progress, growth, and goals. Beginners may need help in thinking more deeply about their teaching. Their own reflection is a powerful vehicle, as is the information you can provide by sensitively discussing their performance with them. The support and information you provide will encourage novices to do more of what is working, grasp and change what is not, and grow in understanding. (If you are a mentor, please take note of the "Note to Mentors" textbox.)

In previous chapters, you explored many facets of teaching that novices must learn and that field-based teacher educators must support. We have focused on your role as a *partner* in new teacher development. The advocacy role continues here, but we expand the focus to include your role as *evaluator*. Chapters 8 and 9 look first at the overall evaluation process and then problems specific to struggling beginners. But here we focus on the skills and understandings you need to observe, analyze, and respond to the beginner's teaching in action. How will you approach this important supervisory task? To begin finding the answer, think a bit about your style. Create a metaphor that captures your supervisory style by completing the following sentence: When it comes to supervising a beginner, I am a _____because_____ _____.

Note to Mentors

This chapter, directed primarily to cooperating teachers, is useful to you especially if your role will include in-class observation and/or evaluation. Here are some things to consider:

- Clarify the district mentorship program's expectations for your involvement in evaluation. Regardless of your role, help your mentee understand the process.
- If the induction program does not require lesson observation, take the initiative and offer to watch a lesson. Feedback is most accepted when it is voluntarily requested and separated from high-stakes decisions (Brinko, 1990).
- Use your post-observation conferences to share the evidence you have gathered through the observation and use reflective conversations to help beginners draw conclusions about their practice.
- Though more experienced than student teachers, beginning teachers may still be uncertain and nervous about your observations. Early efforts to build trusting, collegial relationships will pay off here. As is the case with student teachers, beginners appreciate feedback that is positive, specific, and timely.

What does your answer suggest about your approach to feedback? Are you a *gardener* helping your partner grow? Maybe you are a *flashlight*, there to illuminate the dark corners for your partner. Or perhaps you feel the way these experienced mentors do:

- "I'm a *butterfly*. I kind of flit around and am a little random in my feedback!
- "I am a *stepping stone* that my student teacher can use as she crosses the river into being a teacher."
- "I'm a *hand*—there to lift my student teacher up when he's down and to give him a little push if he needs it!"

Whatever metaphor you choose, your careful feedback will help your partner thrive.

THE POWER OF FEEDBACK

"Make sure you have someone in your life from whom you can get reflective feedback."

—Warren Bennis
(quoted in Creative Quotations, 2002)

Student teachers describe the benefit of ongoing feedback from their cooperating teachers. Giving frequent and sensitive feedback is cited as the single most important action that cooperating teachers take and is the item most missed when it is absent (Guillaume & Rudney, 2002). Student teachers' comments in Box 7.1 remind us that the most helpful feedback is positive, specific, and immediate.

Box 7.1   Student Teachers Comment on Feedback

What's helpful:

"Shari would talk to me and ask me how I thought different parts of the lesson went. I would reflect on what I thought went well and what didn't. Then she would make comments and suggestions on things that she saw. She was always positive and that made feedback effective. I made improvements without feeling bad that I had made mistakes."

"My cooperating teacher provided me with both written and oral feedback. Both of these forms were helpful and effective. We always spoke about the lesson or activity, which was very helpful. She provided me with both positive comments and constructive criticism. I found this most helpful."

What's not:

"[I received] negative feedback only. It was not effective. It was highly discouraging."

"She rarely provided any feedback to me. I even provided her a sheet to fill out after she watched me teach something but I only had one filled out for me. I really do not know how she feels I did this semester."

"There was not much feedback—maybe one or two comments in passing after a lesson. I was reluctant to push after the first two weeks for much of her time as she seemed happiest when I was mostly just taking care of myself."

Cooperating teachers, because of the time they spend with their student teachers, have the greatest opportunity to give informal, ongoing feedback. If your partner skillfully allows students enough time to formulate answers to his or her questions, tell him or her that you notice. Your partner might not even realize it! If your partner successfully includes a distracted student in a discussion, smile and describe the positive aspects of the student's response. Because your partner worries about what you think, the period of time before you have an opportunity to provide feedback after a lesson seems like an eternity. Quickly mention one or two pieces of positive feedback. If you do not have time to chat, briefly jot a note on a slip of paper or in an interactive journal. Informal bits of thoughtful praise are treasures—and often become powerful entries in professional portfolios.

Corrective feedback can also be given informally. In the absence of serious problems, sharing evidence with hints for improvement can help beginners address little problems painlessly. "Did you notice that you had to work to regain

---

Box 7.2   Characteristics of Constructive Feedback

- Describes rather than evaluates

- Is specific rather than general

- Focuses on behavior rather than on the person

SOURCE: Samples from a list originally brainstormed by George Lehner and Al Wright in 1963. Printed in William H. Berquist and Steven R. Phillips's *A Handbook for Faculty Development*, Vol. I (1975, pp. 224–225).

---

their attention? Would having the materials ready to go have encouraged the students to stay with you even longer?" Box 7.2 provides additional guidelines for framing and timing your feedback. Involvement of the mentee in the feedback process is critical. Ask what feedback is most helpful and solicit his or her input and questions. There is no one best time to communicate with your student teacher about performance or issues. Feedback is appropriate before, after, and (sometimes) during lessons.

Before They Teach

Most cooperating teachers find that checking plans weekly or daily is a fruitful way of encouraging student teachers. At all times, try both to encourage and protect the student teacher. Your judgment may be needed to modify an ill-advised lesson but, with guidance and encouragement, your student teacher can meet great challenges. If a fancy or tricky lesson is planned, you can be the safety net. Your mentee may learn from falling . . . and you may be surprised when she *does not* fall. One student teacher remembered her cooperating teacher's reaction to a complicated simulation that she had planned. "My cooperating teacher kind of shook her head and said, 'Well, give it a try.' When it worked, she was happier than I was!" Allowing your mentee the freedom to fail can be viewed as tremendously supportive.

While They Teach

Usually, feedback during a lesson takes the form of nonverbal communication, and it should be positive and supportive. Chapter 5 suggested nonverbal codes so that you and your partner can communicate about the lesson without providing information to the students. During a lesson, your facial expressions, comments, and actions may be perceived as feedback whether you intend them to be or not. A smile or "thumbs up" tells your partner, "You're doing okay!" Experienced observers will recognize a new teacher's look of panic when a mistake has been made. The beginner often glances at the cooperating teacher with a look that says, "Yikes. Do you still think I'm competent?" At this point, a wink or nod gives a tremendous boost. It is easy to misinterpret nonverbal communication and inflate any negative meanings. A frown on your face may have to do with your shoes feeling tight, but your partner may relate it to his or her performance. Try to remain supportive in your use of gestures and facial expressions during a lesson. If possible, keep smiling.

There are times when experienced teachers want to leap into the lesson to help their struggling mentee. In general, *do not do it.* By decreasing the student teacher's confidence or by appearing to undermine the beginner's authority, it can have an effect opposite of what you intend. There are times, however, when student teachers especially may need your help during a lesson, and you should feel comfortable giving it. A supervising teacher recalls a time during her own student teaching when her students were noisily lining up after lunch and she was having trouble getting their attention to quiet them down. Her cooperating teacher moved next to her and whispered, "They can't hear you." That comment made all the difference! She spoke up, and the kids quieted down. The value of the comment extended far beyond the moment. The new teacher realized that volume depended on the situation and that speaking loudly enough to be heard did not equal out-of-control shouting. The cooperating teacher observed, assessed, and provided critical information to improve performance.

Two areas that often require special intervention are discipline and content knowledge. With discipline problems, the best assistance comes before the lesson. For example, you and your partner might decide to allow a student with severe behavioral problems to be a part of the lesson unless he or she becomes a distraction to other students. Remember that your student teacher must learn to manage the classroom on his or her own and that you can intervene when it becomes necessary. The student teacher will learn more by struggling through a difficult situation than by your making everything go smoothly. A little frustration is acceptable. If the frustration gets so intense that he or she is no longer learning, you know you need to help. One student teacher thanked her cooperating teacher both for his willingness to "let me take over and be in control" *and* for "providing assistance when it was needed."

You may also see content errors in your partner's lesson. One student teacher, for example, expressed her embarrassment over a lesson in which she asked young children to describe the earth's three major oceans . . . despite the fact that there are four. Our first advice in this situation is *Wait and see.* First give your partner a little time to catch it and fix it herself. She may have some help from your students—another way to learning. In the ocean example, the student teacher began her next lesson by apologizing for her error and pointing out the four major oceans on a world map.

Most erroneous information can be corrected later but, if it is critical to the students' understanding, sometimes you may have to step in. At this point, our second piece of advice is *A little goes a long way.* A whisper in the ear or a quick note can do the trick. One strong student teacher made a BIG error during a math lesson. Using a pie to describe fractions, she accurately showed half the pie, but when she tried to show sixths, she drew Figure A.

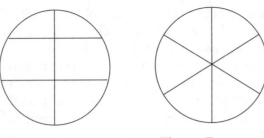

Figure A   **Figure B**

Waiting until the first opportunity to speak privately, her supervisor slipped her a picture of the pie divided into six equal wedges (Figure B) and wrote, "Fractions have to be EQUAL parts." She then said, "You'll need to correct this. Do you have any questions?" All of this was said in private so as not to diminish authority and with the warmest, most supportive demeanor the supervisor could muster. Did the student teacher feel bad? Probably. But this time the supervisor felt it might significantly affect a child's understanding. You will need to make similar judgment calls. Remember to wait and see . . . and that a little goes a long way.

After the Lesson

After a lesson, your partner will be anxious to hear—as soon as possible—your positive and specific feedback. You must balance the delicate tasks of providing the unsupported praise that we all love to hear ("Great lesson!") with providing evidence that allows your partner to draw accurate conclusions about his or her own teaching ("Look at the beautiful drawings they created based on your instruction!"). A reflective conversation, including questions, will help the student teacher work with you in processing the feedback you give. Powerful questions that work well in involving the student teacher are: What did you think? What do you need? What did you notice? Written notes are another good way to give feedback. One cooperating teacher shared her strategy: "Besides the journal, I give immediate feedback after teaching by really quickly writing down notes in two columns labeled 'What Works' and 'Let's Try.' I give a whole list of positives which helps the student teacher build skills to be constantly evaluating her own teaching." Dialogue journals are useful to keep communication open on aspects of teaching that may involve more than a single lesson. Some student teachers appreciate the chance to write their concerns.

Though feedback should be positive, it must be honest and accurate. You help beginners become autonomous when you support them in making their own judgments about their success. Eventually they will be virtually the sole judge of many classroom decisions, and they need support now in making accurate judgments. For example, saying "I like the way you focused kids' attention" makes you the sole judge. Instead, try "Did you notice how every eye was riveted on you when you brought out the crystal at the beginning of the lesson?" It is a good idea to keep the ratio of positive comments to suggestions greater than one-to-one. One student teacher remarked on the importance of pointing out the good with the bad ". . . even if the cooperating teacher has to pull the good thing out of the dark. Because *everything* couldn't be bad."

Your partner will be far more likely to consider your suggestions if she perceives you as fair minded and as an advocate. Use I-statements as one strategy for lowering possible defensiveness when you offer constructive feedback. As one student teacher shared, "It doesn't bother me because of *how* she tells me. She'll say, 'Here are some things I've tried,' and gives me suggestions to try." The use of I-statements by the cooperating teacher made it easier for her student teacher to receive the messages.

Informal, ongoing feedback helps guide beginners toward excellence and helps them maintain their motivation to do well for their students. They want to hear positives and they need to hear suggestions. The more you involve new teacher partners in discussing and reflecting upon their growth, the better they will perform.

FORMAL OBSERVATION

Formal observation and assessment of instruction, usually required by the cooperating university and often part of district mentorship programs, document progress and are a part of assuring fairness, accuracy, and accountability. Your partner will have the opportunity to read and discuss your written feedback, and you can determine together how well your perceptions match. Formal feedback also helps the beginners to be accountable for their performance. As student teachers read, understand, and discuss the feedback given in formal settings, they understand the expectations that they will have to meet. You, the student teacher, and the university supervisor can identify and discuss areas of strength and weakness and formulate specific goals for improvement. The written record of your student teacher's growth and competence is the evidence that you and the university supervisor will need in your role as gatekeepers. Should this student teacher be credentialed to teach? The formal feedback you help to compile supports your answer to that important question.

Mentor teachers often participate in the formative assessment part of the overall evaluation system and are freed from making high-stakes decisions. If you are a district mentor, you will provide feedback and support aimed at improvement. Usually the responsibility for summative assessment and decision making rests with the principal.

Whatever your specific role, the first *formal* lesson observation can provoke anxiety both for your partner *and* for you. To get you thinking about the experience, complete the following exercise.

The First Observation!

Joe Thompson is in his third week of student teaching in your sixth-grade classroom. He is always on time in the morning. You have noticed that he is timid but pleasant. At 23, he is very bright and has come well prepared for his beginning duties in your classroom. Tomorrow during social studies, he will teach an inquiry lesson (where students will make educated guesses from data), and he seems nervous about his questioning technique. You will observe the lesson and want to have a planning session today.

Think and write about how you intend to approach the session and what you might want to bring up as issues or concerns.

Does your plan reflect the supervisory metaphor you developed earlier in the chapter? In the following subsections, we present three approaches to supervision, each with deep roots within particular paradigms of research and theory, and each with an implied supervisory metaphor: supervisor as scientist, sculptor, or coach.

Scientific Approach

The scientific approach provides feedback and compares the teacher's performance to a predetermined standard. You may have been observed by supervisors using this approach. After observing your lesson, the supervisor would probably have rated your performance on a checklist of teaching behaviors related to effective practice, such as the degree to which you specified a clear objective at the beginning of the lesson.

The heart of this model (see Box 7.3) is the belief that *effective teaching* can be captured in a list of specific behaviors or characteristics. The notion is drawn from a long line of teaching research that uses what is called the *process/product paradigm*. In this paradigm, researchers examine particular teaching behaviors or practices (process) and their effects on student learning (product). Among the teacher behaviors and classroom practices valued—and therefore frequently the focus of observation—are adjustment of instruction based on student response, time on task, lesson pacing, effective questioning, clear communication, and active, equal participation by students (see Good & Brophy, 1994, for comprehensive information).

If you follow the scientific model as a supervisor, you will usually focus on specific teaching characteristics that the university or induction program has asked you to identify, often on an observation record. One benefit of the approach is that it allows you to focus on several important teaching characteristics quickly. It may remind you to observe things otherwise overlooked. The approach benefits the beginner by providing clear expectations and allowing for specific feedback on many instructional elements. There are also drawbacks. Though it gives the appearance of science, checklist ratings can lack reliability. Often, what is *excellent* to one observer is only *satisfactory* to another. Sometimes, a lesson does not necessarily fit all of the characteristics listed. Or a set of high or low ratings may not seem to capture what was important about the observed lesson. Particularly if a rating was low, beginners deserve explanation, encouragement, and instruction. Finally, it can

---

Box 7.3   Summary of Scientific Supervision

- Focuses on teaching *behaviors* correlated to student learning
- Draws from a large body of process/product research on teacher effectiveness
- Includes *time on task, active student participation,* and *equitable distribution of questions* as elements associated with important concepts
- Compares the teacher against a predetermined standard
- Uses checklists to record the presence and quality of specified skills

SOURCE: Drawn from the work of McNeil (1982)

---

be all too easy to rely on fairly general checkmarks instead of the personal, specific feedback that is so useful in improving performance and boosting confidence.

Artistic Supervision

Rather than viewing teaching as a science, a supervisor can view teaching as an art. Artistic supervision, summarized in Box 7.4, allows a more holistic view of your mentee's style and performance in the classroom. This approach allows you to look beyond lists of discrete teaching skills to discover the strengths, motivations, and meanings present in your partner's instruction. Ultimately, your goal as supervisor is to help your partner exploit those strengths by building on positive actions already in place. You observe with an open mind, looking for particularly meaningful or illustrative incidents. Rather than measuring teaching behaviors against a fixed standard, you seek first to understand the salient features of your partner's style and then to help him or her understand it in terms of excellent teaching.

Once you have formulated an interpretation of your partner's style, you need to help him or her perceive, appreciate, and strengthen its positive aspects. To do so, the artistic approach often uses narrative language or the language of story. Sometimes, the artistic supervisor uses metaphor to convey the heart of the teacher's teaching style. Unaware of being able to answer student questions, pass out materials, calm an overly excited student, and keep smiling all at the same time, your student teacher would be happy to hear you describe him or her as a capable and cheerful juggler!

In this approach, the supervisor *as artist* looks for the essence of the teacher's style to emerge (see Box 7.4). You will be observant and analytical, avoiding quick judgments. Your written communication with your partner will usually take the form of narrative writing rich in description. The benefits of this approach include the freedom for you to identify and encourage development of observed strengths. You will not be limited to a tidy, but perhaps inadequate, list of skills. This approach allows for very positive communications with the beginner. Beginners benefit from thoughtful descriptions of their work. They benefit also from the approach's flexibility in giving them helpful feedback appropriate to their level of professional development.

Box 7.4   Summary of Artistic Supervision

- Focuses on the *meaning* of classroom incidents and behaviors
- Notices what *is* occuring and considers what *ought* to be occuring
- Uses sensitivity and knowledge of teaching to understand the student teacher's personal style
- *Perceives, appreciates,* and *strengthens* subtle and postive aspects of personal style
- Uses narrative to describe the student teacher's style in rich, descriptive detail

SOURCE: Drawn from the work of Eisner (1982)

Artistic supervision has its drawbacks. In capturing the *essence* of a teacher's style and strengths, supervisors may fail to alert partners to standards of practice that are missing from their performance. We do have a knowledge base in our profession, and novices need to think about their teaching and how it fits with what we believe expert teachers do. In particular, mentees experiencing difficulty may not get the specific feedback necessary to correct deficiencies in their teaching. Finally, this approach requires a high degree of skill on the part of the mentor. The experienced partner must be able to observe, conceptualize, and write with clarity and compassion.

Clinical Supervision

Clinical supervision, summarized in Box 7.5, is a *process* model with a clear focus on collaboration between supervisor and supervisee. It focuses on teachers' classroom performance and is based on the belief that teachers will learn better and more positively when the supervision is responsive to their own concerns. Thus, the novice is an *active* participant in the process. In clinical supervision, supervisors and their partners work *together* to determine the focus of observation and to plan for improvement. Usually, the model proceeds in the following three stages: the *planning conference,* the *classroom observation,* and the *feedback conference.*

First, the supervisor and partner have a *planning conference.* Your role at this conference is to solicit your partner's needs, concerns, or even aspirations. A key question to ask at this meeting is "What would you like me to observe during this lesson?" When your partner states his or her needs or concerns, you discuss and decide what to observe and how best to record the data. You need to determine a way to address the stated concerns using observable data. For example, many student teachers are concerned about classroom control. One author remembers a student teacher who knew exactly what she wanted to know. She asked for the supervisor to tell her "what the students are doing that I do *not* notice." To make it observable and objective, they agreed that any student misbehavior noticed would be listed in one column and, in a second column, the supervisor would list the student teacher's response.

There are many methods of simple data recording. You might try writing verbatim records of preselected interactions, using seating charts to record behavior or verbal

---

Box 7.5   Summary of Clinical Supervision

- Focuses on teachers' classroom performance
- Is a *process* approach characterized by *collaboration, collegiality,* and *professionalism*
- Includes the novice as an active part of the process
- Proceeds in three phases: planning conference, classroom observation, and feedback conference
- Hopes to foster teachers' inquiry into their own professional growth

SOURCE: Drawn from the work of Acheson and Gall (1992) and Garman (1982)

flow, making anecdotal records, or using other coding schemes. For detailed explanations of possible techniques, read *Techniques in the Clinical Supervision of Teachers* by Acheson and Gall (1992).

The second stage is the *classroom observation.* Here, your job is to watch carefully and make notes using the selected data-gathering method. You will also want to notice other important classroom occurrences, but usually you should maintain the predetermined focus. A classroom teacher remembered one of her experiences during student teaching. She had worked hard on her lesson opening or anticipatory set and asked her supervisor to watch it and give her feedback. After the lesson, the supervisor told her about one child who didn't understand the lesson and two who were off task during the project and so on. The former student teacher remembered thinking in frustration, "But how was the *SET?*" Because this is a collaborative model, it is important to honor the decisions you make together.

The last stage is the post-observation or *feedback conference.* This conference, preferably scheduled soon after the observation, allows you and your new teacher partner to review the lesson and plan for improvement. Usually you can let the data record speak for itself. In the case of the student teacher who worried about what she *did not* notice, the chart did reveal the behaviors she did not seem to address. By looking at the data, she concluded that she actually *did* notice the misbehaviors but was very uncomfortable and inconsistent with disciplining certain students. The observer did not need to tell her; she could see it for herself. Planning for improvement often requires a little more direction from the observer. If there is a problem, the student teacher can be very discouraged. As one student teacher explained, "If I *knew* what to do, I'd *do* it!" In keeping with the collaborative nature of this model (see Box 7.5), you need to work with your partner to put the data and the interpretation of the data in the context of your classroom and his or her relative inexperience. Do not be afraid to make suggestions, but remember to brainstorm possible ideas, solutions, or strategies *together.*

There are, of course, drawbacks to the clinical supervision model. The process is time consuming, as many important things are. Also, a detailed and thought-consuming collection of a particular kind of data in answer to a particular question may result in selective perception and avert attention from a different critical element in the lesson, one that may be more important. In every approach, skill, sensitivity, and good sense are needed to meet the needs of the beginning teacher.

LOOKING AHEAD

In this chapter, we focus on providing feedback with an assumption that beginners are doing adequate work. The same strategies and approaches apply if your partner is struggling, but future chapters will address those special situations. Giving observation and feedback,

"In the field of observation, chance favors the prepared mind."

—Louis Pasteur
(quoted in Creative Quotations, 2002)

whether formal or informal, whether positive or negative, is a *shared* experience. Success and appreciation grow when mentees feel valued and actively involved. Your relationship with university or district personnel will also be stronger when ideas and experiences are shared.

EXERCISES

Exercise 7.1   Joe's First Lesson Observation

This case study tells the story of Joe, a student teacher who experiences his first formal lesson observation. You met Joe as he prepared for this lesson when you completed "The First Observation!" box earlier in this chapter. This narrative is designed to promote thoughtful discussion. Analyze the instructional event from the perspectives of both the student teacher and the cooperating teacher.

1. Read the case quickly to get the story. Read it again slowly to identify issues that are present.

2. Answer the questions that follow the case study. Discuss them with your student teacher.

3. The greatest benefit of a case study is found in *discussing* it. Find a small group of teachers to read and discuss this case. If there are several cooperating teachers at your site, perhaps the case could be part of a faculty meeting.

Joe's First Lesson Observation

Joe Thompson skimmed his lesson plan one last time. As a student teacher for a sixth-grade class, he wanted everything to go right. Today, Karen Dutton, his cooperating teacher, would be formally observing his lesson for the first time. Joe hated to admit it, but he was nervous. He would have preferred for Karen to see his math class because he felt much more comfortable in math. Karen had told him that she had made math her top priority this year, and he felt really comfortable with the routine she had established. Karen, however, had suggested that she watch this lesson first, and he did not ask for anything different. In all honesty, he felt funny requesting the change. He did not want her to think that he was uncooperative. He didn't want to rock the boat.

Joe felt support from all corners. When he first attended the teacher workshops in September, he was welcomed warmly. Karen had shown him around the school and introduced him to her colleagues, who had talked and joked with him and had promised to give him any help he needed. They had made good on their promises. Joe figured he must have the best placement of any student teacher. His university supervisor had told him how well she thought he would do with Karen and now, three weeks into the placement, he was sure she was right.

Joe had to laugh at himself. He was having a great experience, but he was still nervous about the observation. Well, like he told the high school girls on the volleyball team he coached, "Just go out there and do your job. The butterflies in your stomach will take care of themselves." Good advice, Joe thought to himself.

Karen sat down in the back of the classroom about five minutes before the lesson was supposed to start. "Well, Joe, are you ready?" As always, she was professional but friendly. "Do you have a copy of the lesson plan for me?" Joe gave Karen his plans and hoped she liked them. He glanced again at the first part of the plan, the dreaded objectives:

1. The students will work in groups to solve problems.

2. The students will practice inductive thinking skills by observing, inferring, and formulating hypotheses on a given set of data.

3. The students will state the generalization: "Though the communication may take different forms, all cultures communicate."

He hoped that these were what she was looking for. Karen must have seen his concern. "I like to know where you're headed, even if you don't get there!" Karen said, laughing.

Joe started to relax a bit. Karen was supportive. "You'll see me taking notes, but don't be worried. I want to remember any hints I'll have for you when we talk afterward. This is going to be fun for me!"

"I hope that it's fun for both of us!" Joe joked as he began to welcome the class back from lunch recess.

The students entered noisily but quickly. Joe greeted them: "Good job, kids! I hope you had a good lunch. I'll be teaching your social studies lesson today. I hope you like it."

The kids turned in their seats to look at Mrs. Dutton. She gave a quick wave and then turned her attention to Joe. The class followed her lead, and Joe began his lesson.

"You've been studying colonial times for a while, but today we're going to look at the people who were here long before the colonists ever came. Who was already here?"

"Columbus," called out Greg from the back of the room. There were a few giggles from the other students.

"Okay. Columbus, of course, had been to the Caribbean Islands in, you all know the year . . . ."

"1492!" shouted a chorus of students.

"Right. 1492. And he first discovered America . . . or at least brought . . . or made known to Europe that there was another continent. But who was already here?"

"The Vikings." It was Greg again.

"Okay—you're right, Greg. Some people believe that the Vikings were here even before Columbus arrived, but I think you know what I'm going for here. Who was already here?" Joe felt the butterflies return. He glanced at Karen, who was busily writing notes. "Gretchen?"

"There were already Indians here."

"Exactly. There were many different groups of native people living all over the continents of North and South America long before any of the European explorers arrived. Good.

"Today, we're going to do some detective work. We're going to pretend that you are early colonists to North America, among the first Europeans here. You've begun looking for a place to build your first shelter. You know you have to hurry because you want to survive the winter. You find a place, and then you find a tree that you're going to cut down for wood. But on the tree, you notice some strange carvings.

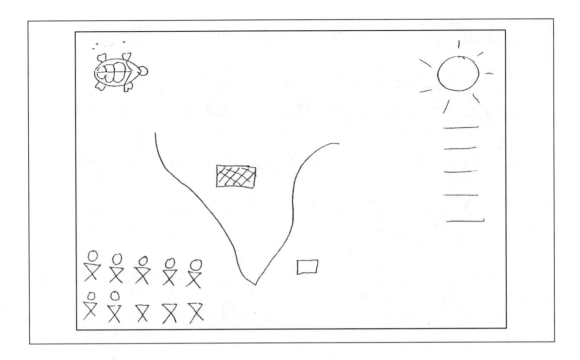

"In your normal groups now, the ones you use for math, look at this worksheet that shows the carvings that you have found on that tree. What you want to do is figure out what the carvings mean."

The students quickly adjusted their desks so that they were in their groups of four. Joe was pleased that they seemed eager to see the Indian pictographs. He had written this lesson for his social studies methods class at the university, and his professor had really liked it. He hadn't had much practice with the inquiry strategy that he was going to try, but he wanted something more interesting than the textbook work that he had seen the class using regularly.

"Okay, class. Here's what I want you to do. First, I want you to write down everything you *observe* in the tree carvings. We're pretending these are the real carvings. Like you see a sun. Write that down. Okay? We'll take a few minutes for you to make your lists. You are . . . like . . . writing down the data."

The groups worked intently for several minutes. Joe moved among the groups encouraging the students or just observing. The students did not ask many questions, and he was pleased. "Okay, guys. Let's get back together here. Everybody face front. Excellent. Let's write our data as a group. What did you observe?" Each group volunteered items from their lists, and soon the board contained a master list:

Sun

Turtle

5 lines

People

People without heads

2 long curved lines

2 squares

"Good. Now that we have carefully looked at the information, we want to use our detective skills. What do these pictures mean? In your groups, I want you to look at the data and make some educated guesses about what the pictures mean. Who carved them? Why?" This time, as Joe moved from group to group, the kids seemed confused. "What do you want, Mr. Thompson? We don't know what these pictures are," said Sarah, who seemed to be speaking for her whole group and others in the class as well.

Joe decided to explain to the whole group one more time. "Everybody, let's look to the front again. We seem to be having a little more trouble with this step. Let's go over it again. You've looked carefully at the carvings. Now you're making a guess about what they mean. We don't know, but we're guessing." Sarah's hand went up. "Sarah?"

"Do you know what they mean?" Sarah asked innocently enough. The class waited for Mr. Thompson's answer.

"Yeah. I know what they mean," Joe tried to explain patiently. "But we don't just want to know what they mean; we want to practice figuring out what they mean. We want to think about the data, the facts, the carvings, and then make some guesses about the meanings. We may not get it exactly right, but if our guesses make sense they'll be good ones.

"Let's try one together. Aaron, what do you think the picture of the sun might mean?" Joe smiled encouragingly at Aaron and stole a glance at Karen. Just watching, he thought. He was not sure what she was thinking.

"It's the sun," replied Aaron.

"Right. It's the sun, but who knows what it might *mean?*" Joe hoped he didn't sound desperate.

"Do you mean like a *day?*" volunteered Eric.

"Yes! That's the idea! Maybe the Indians were telling us something about how many days or that it was daytime . . . something like that. Do you think you can work in your groups now?"

The students nodded or voiced quietly their understanding. They turned back to their groups and began talking. Joe felt much better as he listened to the different groups working now. The kids were so willing to work. He loved to hear their ideas. The lesson is going well, he thought.

Joe brought the attention of the group back to the front once again. "I'd like to hear some of your interpretations before we go on to the next step of the lesson. Amanda, what things did your group say?"

"Well," said Amanda quietly, "we thought that the turtle might mean that the Indians were taking a slow trip." Her group giggled, and Amanda's face turned red. "And we thought the people without heads were dead." Many students began to giggle.

"Okay. Now, let's stay focused here. Those were interesting ideas. Anybody else?"

Greg spoke up, "We thought that the dead people had been eaten by a giant turtle from outer space." Greg laughed. Everybody laughed. Even Karen, Joe noticed.

"You students are creative. That's good." Joe smiled broadly. "But without ruining our fun here, I'd like you to think again about our goal. We want to make our *best*, most *educated* guess about what these symbols mean. Who do we think probably carved these symbols in the tree?"

Joe smiled as the students responded, "Indians."

"Right. And you know what? This set of pictures was really found carved in a tree. So we're trying to figure out, to decipher, a real message. So if we're trying to make the *best* guess possible, what do we think the turtle might symbolize or mean? Greg?"

"I guess we'd think it meant slow journey, but I still think ours is better."

"Well, I can appreciate that. In a creative or fun way, yours is better maybe. But in our analytical way, the other is better. Do you all know what I mean?" Joe started to worry. Should he have said that? Was he supposed to accept every answer because he had just asked them to make guesses? He began to wonder if he should have invited Karen to see his math class instead.

"For the last step of our lesson, you will write out the entire meaning of the message. You have already discussed possible meanings for each symbol, but now, in your groups, write out the meaning of the message as if it were a story. First, talk about the things that you want to say in the story and the order you'll want to say them. Then, pick one person to work as the recorder, just like we do in math, and work together to write a draft of the story. I'll be around to help you if you need it."

After a few questions, all of the groups got down to work. Joe visited Greg's group right away. "You know, if you want, you can write one story that is your best guess and then write another crazy story about turtles from outer space. How does that sound?" The kids smiled and got down to work.

Joe turned his attention to Karen. "Well?" said Joe. "What do you think?"

"It was really interesting, Joe!" Karen smiled reassuringly. "I have to leave now for the staff meeting, but we'll discuss it right after school. I'm really anxious to see how *you* thought you did."

As Joe turned his attention back to the class, he couldn't stop thinking about what Karen would have to say.

- What are Joe's strengths? His growth areas?
- How well does Joe teach his lesson? What did he do well? How might he have done better? What problems did he fail to anticipate? What is your evidence for each of your conclusions?
- How should Karen evaluate the lesson?
- What does Karen think of the lesson?
- What goals might Karen have for Joe's first "official" lesson?
- What does she know about Joe and how does she know it?
- What will she learn from the observation and conference?
- If Karen knows about inquiry and knows about assisting student teachers, what should she say to Joe?

Exercise 7.2   Practicing the Scientific Approach

In this and the next two exercises, you will practice each of the three approaches discussed in this chapter by reading a case study and evaluating the lesson described in it. We know that it is hard to evaluate a teacher from a short case study, but it is a beginning.

1. Read the case study in Exercise 7.1, Joe's First Lesson Observation. Try to picture the lesson in your head and complete the following chart.

2. If possible, share the assessment with your partner and compare answers. Does your cooperating university have a "scientifically-based" evaluation form? How does it compare to the sample form below?

3. Analyze the scientific approach. What qualities of teaching did it enable you to observe? What elements of the approach did you like? Dislike? What made it easier or more difficult than other approaches?

Lesson Aspects Observed	Superior	Good	Adequate	Weak	Not Observed
Opening of lesson motivates students.					
Objective of lesson and directions are clear.					
Questions or problems anticipated.					
Attention of students maintained.					
Routine matters handled efficiently.					
Rapport with students developed.					
Objective of lesson met.					
Demonstrates competency in leading whole class or group discussions.					
Gives appropriate feedback.					

Exercise 7.3   Practicing the Artistic Approach

Now get a taste for the artistic approach and see how it might work for you. This exercise, when done well, may take more time than Exercise 7.2, but we think it is worth it.

1. Read the case study found in Exercise 7.1, Joe's First Lesson Observation. Picture the lesson in your head and try to formulate a clear notion of Joe as a teacher. Answer the following questions:

   - What does Joe do that seems to be unique or distinctive?

   - What do you especially appreciate in Joe's teaching?

   - What suggestions would you make to reinforce the values and characteristics of his teaching that are part of teaching excellence?

   - What metaphor might you use to describe Joe's teaching?

2. Write a one-page report that you would share with Joe. Remember to use a narrative form and build on positives.

3. Think about the questions in relation to your own partner. What are his or her special gifts? How can you build on them?

4. Analyze the artistic approach. What qualities of teaching were you able to observe? What elements of the approach did you like? Dislike? What made it easier or more difficult than others?

Exercise 7.4 Practicing the Clinical Approach

This is the last exercise for Joe's lesson, and you will have the opportunity to practice the observation phase of the clinical approach.

1. Read the following explanation of the initial conference and study the chart that was devised to organize the data you will collect to give feedback to Joe on his questioning strategies.

2. Complete the chart based on evidence found in Exercise 7.1, Joe's First Observation.

3. Analyze the completed chart. What suggestions will you make during the final conference with Joe? What questions might he have?

4. Try to role play the final conference with your student teacher.

5. Actually follow the three-phase format for one of your partner's lessons. Be sure to "objectify" the question so that your main job during the observation will be to collect data.

6. Analyze the clinical approach. What qualities of teaching were you able to observe using it? What elements of the approach did you like? Dislike? What made it easier or more difficult than other approaches?

During the pre-observation conference, Joe discussed his interest in improving questioning strategies. The two of you decided to evaluate the lesson by listing each question, student response, and Joe's follow-up response.

Teacher Question	Student Response	Follow-up
Who was already here?	Greg: Columbus	Okay. Columbus, of course, had been to the Caribbean Islands . . . .

8

Summative Evaluation

"It is disconcerting for me to be in the position where my decision can have tremendous impact on someone's life and career. I suppose that I have to take each case, each decision at a time. I have to examine as many facts as I can. I have to look for my biases and try to evaluate as objectively as possible. And then I have to live with the decision that I make. But it isn't easy."

—A cooperating teacher

As a teacher, you already know about evaluation, the process of appraising performance and making judgments about its quality. You know that good evaluation cannot come just at the end without feedback along the way. You know that final evaluation must be linked to what has been taught. You know that the results of the final, or *summative*, evaluation can have profound effects on your students. You may have experienced the excitement of assigning a final grade that reveals to a student the positive results of hard work. You may have experienced the agony of assigning a low grade to a student who tried hard (and for whom *you* tried hard) but just couldn't meet minimum standards.

We know that new teacher partners want faith, freedom, and feedback from their mentors, and we have discussed many ways to provide it. Whereas most new and experienced mentors report high levels of comfort and confidence with the supportive coaching role, they—like the cooperating teacher whose comments you read above—find evaluation the most difficult aspect of supervision. This chapter addresses a critical—and sometimes troubling—duty for mentors: that of providing fair, comprehensive, and meaningful final evaluation to preservice or first-year teachers. Begin by considering the answers to the following key questions:

- Who are key players in the final evaluation of your mentees?
- What are the criteria on which your mentee will be evaluated?

- When are evaluation checkpoints best scheduled?
- Where will final evaluations be placed and who will have access to them?
- Why is the summative evaluation important to your student teacher?
- How should you complete an effective summative evaluation?

Evaluation and support systems are in place for preservice and first-year teachers. Cooperating teachers will most certainly play a role in the university's system as they give summative evaluation for their student teachers' performances during student teaching. Mentors may participate in their district's evaluation process as well, but typically their role is as a provider of formative assessment and support. Think about your specific roles, responsibilities, and needs as we explore the concepts, procedures, and expectations for evaluation of preservice and beginning teachers.

THE LOGIC OF EVALUATION

Four steps outline a logical process of assessment that can be applied to any system of evaluation in which a judgment of value must be made (Shadish, 1998). Essentially, the four steps require evaluators to

1. Determine what will be judged.

2. Establish the comparative and absolute standards of performance.

3. Gather relevant data.

4. Integrate results into final judgment.

An examination of the four steps implemented in teacher evaluation provides important background for you as you meet the demands of your evaluator role.

What Will Be Judged?

> "A teacher affects eternity; he can never tell where his influence stops."
>
> —Henry Brooks Adams
> (quoted in Creative Quotations, 2002)

To determine the focus of evaluation in teacher education, we ask "What is good teaching?" The answers to that question have included elements of moral character, personality traits, specific behaviors, cognition, and reflections of teachers, as well as teacher impact on student learning (Barrett, 1986). Danielson and McGreal (2000) suggest that a shift from behaviorist to constructivist views has allowed teachers to develop personal views of good teaching with the result that teachers share fewer values and assumptions. Yet, in what Darling-Hammond (1996) calls a quiet revolution, the teaching profession has engaged in standard setting that reflects a knowledge base and consensus about what teachers should know and do to ensure that all students learn. Yinger (1999) describes the powerful consensus three premier professional educational associations have established in defining and assessing good teaching throughout a career. These three associations—the National Council for the Accreditation of Teachers (NCATE), the Interstate New Teacher Assessment and Support Consortium (INTASC), and the National Board for Professional Teaching Standards (NBPTS)—have formulated the standards that are listed in Table 8.1. Notice the image of professional teachers as "knowledgeable, reflective practitioners,

Table 8.1   Standards of Teaching Excellence

INTASC	NBPTS
Teachers: - Understand the subjects they teach and make them meaningful to students. - Understand how children learn and develop, and can provide learning opportunities that support their growth. - Understand how students differ and create instructional opportunities adapted to student need. - Understand and use a variety of instructional strategies to encourage development of critical thinking, problem solving and performance skills. - Understand group and individual motivation and behavior to create a learning environment that encourages positive social interaction, active engagement in learning, and self-motivation. - Use knowledge of effective communication techniques to foster inquiry, collaboration, and supportive interaction. - Plan instruction based on knowledge of subject matter, students, the community, and curricular goals. - Understand and use formal and informal assessment strategies to evaluate and ensure continuous intellectual, social and physical development of the learner. - Are reflective practitioners who continually evaluate the effects of choices and actions on others and who actively seek out opportunities to grow professionally. - Foster relationships with colleagues and community to support student learning and well-being. SOURCE: INTASC (1992)	Teachers: - Are committed to student learning. - Know the subject matter they teach and how to teach those subjects to students. - Are responsible for managing and monitoring student learning. - Think systematically about their practice and learn from experience. - Are members of learning communities. SOURCE: NBPTS (2002)
	NCATE
	"Candidates preparing to work in schools as teachers or other professional school personnel know and demonstrate the content, pedagogical, and professional knowledge, skills, and dispositions necessary to help all students learn. Assessments indicate that candidates meet professional, state, and institutional standards." SOURCE: NCATE (2001, p. 10)

willing and able to engage in collaborative, contextually grounded learning activities." (Yinger, 1999, p. 103). We have a sense of what to judge. What standards does your university, district, or state use? How do they relate to national standards?

Setting Standards of Performance

Now we answer this question: What is good . . . and what is good enough? Evaluators must determine or establish the criteria that capture the quality of knowledge or performance. Without criteria, assessment tasks may be nothing more than interesting or instructional activities (Herman, Aschbacher, & Winters, 1992). Establishing criteria will clarify and make public the expected and acceptable standards for performance. Those who will be evaluated—always, but especially when the stakes are high— need to know what is good . . . and good enough. Establishing and understanding criteria are necessary "because they help you judge complex human performance in a reliable, fair, and valid manner" (Herman et al., 1992, p. 46).

For teacher evaluation, criteria are often presented in rubrics that offer descriptions of teacher performance at different skill levels. Rubrics attempt to describe what "good" teaching looks like and should be tied to policies and standards (Carr & Harris, 2001). Table 8.2 shows, for example, the rubric used to judge the content knowledge standard for graduates of NCATE accredited teacher education programs (NCATE, 2001). Though broad, the criteria suggest key differences in levels of performance.

Other frameworks for evaluation of classroom teaching are available. Danielson (1996), for example, divided the complex activity of teaching into four domains: planning and preparation, classroom environment, instruction, and professional responsibilities. The four domains were further divided into 22 total components, which were then broken down further into elements within the components. Danielson has devised a detailed rubric specific to each element. A sample rubric, summarizing in general the tenor of her descriptors, is provided in Table 8.3. The descriptors illustrate differences in quality for teachers whose performance is either unsatisfactory, basic, proficient or distinguished.

These and other statements of criteria help evaluators to differentiate between acceptable and unacceptable performance. What criteria have your university or

Table 8.2 NCATE Content Knowledge Standard for Teacher Candidates

Unacceptable	Acceptable	Target
Have inadequate knowledge of subject matter they plan to teach as shown by their inability to give examples of important principles or concepts delineated in professional, state, and institutional standards. Unable to give examples of important principles or concepts.	Know the subject matter they plan to teach as shown by their ability to explain important principles and concepts delineated in professional, state, and institutional standards.	Have in-depth knowledge of the subject matter they plan to teach as described in professional, state, and institutional standards. They demonstrate their knowledge through inquiry, critical analysis, and synthesis of subject.

SOURCE: NCATE (2001)

Table 8.3 General Rubric for Elements of Teaching

Unsatisfactory	Basic	Proficient	Distinguished
• Does *not* yet appear to understand relevant concepts. • Work on fundamental practices will enable growth and development.	• *Appears* to understand relevant concepts. • Attempts to implement elements. • Implementation is not entirely successful. • Reading, discussion, classroom visitations, and support from mentor enable growth. • Minimally competent with little or no harm to students.	• *Clearly* understands relevant concepts. • Implements those concepts well. • Most experienced, capable teachers are considered to be at this level.	• Master teacher who contributes to the field, both in and outside school. • Qualitatively different from classrooms of less-skilled or less-proficient teachers. • Creates community of learners, with motivated students who assume responsibility for their own learning.

SOURCE: Drawn from the work of Danielson (1996)

district established? How are the criteria communicated to the people who will be evaluated? As mentors, you are *teachers* as well as assessors. As such, you will collaborate with your mentees to devise goals and learning experiences based on the relevant standards and criteria for good teaching.

Data and Documentation

With standards and criteria established, evaluators next gather data and documentation. Data, carefully aligned to goals, allow evaluators to determine a fair and supportable assessment—and to provide information that those who are evaluated can use to draw conclusions of their own.

As mentors, you will make instructional and evaluative decisions about several different professional elements. Just as instruction should align with goals, so should assessment sources. It is important to collect different kinds of information. Experts suggest obtaining a wide variety of evidence, including

> "If you get all the facts, your judgment can be right; if you don't get all the facts, it can't be right."
>
> —Bernard Baruch
> (quoted in Creative Quotations, 2002)

Table 8.4 Data Sources

Written Documents	Observations and Interactions
• Lesson and unit plans • Written evaluations of student learning after teaching • Samples of student work • Written self-assessments • Materials created for lessons • Reflective writing • Letters to parents • Newsletters • Portfolio • Log of professional development activities	• Relationship with children • Interaction with colleagues or other school personnel • Feedback from colleagues, parents or students • Surveys • Interviews • Formal lesson observations • Behavioral checklists (see Exercise 7.2 in Chapter 7 for an example of such a checklist). • Analyses of videotaped lessons

teacher-generated artifacts, formal and informal observations, feedback from others, and behavioral checklists (Danielson & McGreal, 2000; Herman et al., 1992). Table 8.4 provides a sampling of data sources.

In addition to collecting a variety of data, supervisors need to ensure that the data is collected—and shared—over time. This practice has multiple benefits. First, it assures ample opportunity for your mentee to set goals and meet requirements. Second, it allows you to establish a collaborative relationship geared to improving learning for students. Third, it allows you to see a pattern of behavior and have greater faith in your ongoing and ultimate judgments. Finally, it provides written documentation of your findings, your communication with the mentee, and your efforts to assist in the mentee's growth and development. Early in your supervisory experience, examine the required form or structure of the summative evaluation. What key goals will your partner strive to meet and will you be asked to judge? For each, create a list of possible evidence. Collect evidence for each at the beginning, in the middle, and at the end of the experience.

Making Data-Based Final Judgments

> "True genius resides in the capacity for evaluation of uncertain, hazardous, and conflicting information."
>
> —Winston Churchill (quoted in Creative Quotations, 2002)

When it comes time for the final evaluation, you will have already been using your assessment data for ongoing feedback, goal setting, and perhaps instruction. The last evaluative step is to examine data, analyze findings, and make a final judgment. For cooperating teachers and others who are responsible for summative evaluations, this is an essential and critical step. Cooperating teachers' final assessments may affect their student teachers' employment opportunities and in some cases even their ability to obtain teaching credentials. Luckily, most teacher education programs have an assessment system in place and field-based evaluators are only one part of it—albeit an important one. Summative judgments at institutions that meet NCATE's target level for assessment meet the following standards:

Decisions about candidate performance are based on multiple assessments made at multiple points before program completion. Data show the strong relationship of performance assessments to candidate success. The unit conducts thorough studies to establish fairness, accuracy, and consistency of its performance assessment procedures. (NCATE, 2001, p. 21)

Supervisors must understand and manage several features of evaluation to ensure that summative judgments are as fair, accurate, and defensible as possible. As experienced evaluators of students, you are familiar with the concepts of validity, reliability, and bias. Here we offer a quick refresher on these critical concepts for your role as evaluator of teachers.

- *Validity.* Put simply, validity means that an evaluation tool or method measures what it purports to measure. Teacher evaluation is valid if it incorporates what is important about teaching (Danielson, 1996). Face validity means that the evaluation tools appear, in the opinion of knowledgeable professionals, to match what is important. Validity is also determined by comparing a measure with other established guidelines. That standards established by different professional organizations are similar adds to their validity. Appropriate choice of data sources is essential to valid assessment.

- *Reliability.* Reliability refers to consistency and trustworthiness in measurement. Herman et al. (1992) explain that an assessment is reliable if several judges looking at a task performance would come to the same conclusion and would rate the performance about the same on a subsequent occasion. Reliability also requires that the performance observed is representative of a pattern of behavior. To assure that summative evaluations of preservice or first-year teachers are reliable, data should be triangulated through multiple data sources and multiple judges. More than one person should have input, and judgments should be comparable, thus demonstrating *interrater agreement*. Training, communication, and collaboration can help establish consistency because raters need a common vision and similar understanding of criteria. Danielson (1996) adds that reliability, though important for mentoring and coaching, is essential for the high-stakes environment. Questions to ask include these: Do different pieces of evidence support the same judgment? Do other evaluators notice similar strengths and weaknesses? Are lessons successfully implemented in all subject areas?

- *Controlling bias.* To provide accurate assessment and evaluation, supervisors must try to avoid being influenced by personal opinion. Though your professional knowledge of standards and expectations for beginning teachers is the basis for your evaluation, subjectivity is inherent in the process, and you must work to limit its control and influence (Cruickshank, Bainer, & Metcalf, 1999). Gay (1992) describes two problems often associated with rating scales (and which are frequently present in teacher evaluation). The halo effect refers to a phenomenon where overall feelings toward the person being evaluated or feelings about one aspect of their performance cause the evaluator to raise scores in other areas. A similar phenomenon is the generosity error—the tendency to give the benefit of the doubt to the person being rated. Danielson and McGreal (2000) believe that bias can best be controlled by using behaviorally anchored rating scales (see Exercise 7.2 in Chapter 7 for an example) and including narrative feedback. A well-written narrative allows for extended and more fully described explanations of evaluative judgments.

Studies of student teaching evaluations reveal that judgments are usually high regardless of the instrument used (Barrett, 1986). The generosity error may cause supervisors to evaluate potential rather than actual performance. Also, if it is true that student teachers often adopt the style of their cooperating teachers, it could lead to higher ratings. Both cooperating teachers and university supervisors seem to share the desire to protect student teachers from risk and make them as comfortable as possible (Borko & Mayfield, 1995). In addition to the halo effect and the generosity error, plausible explanations for highly positive evaluations include solid preparation prior to student teaching and a well-functioning system of evaluation that results in the withdrawal of students who are performing poorly.

Evaluators examine the data carefully collected over time, work to control assessment errors, and make the best, most accurate summative evaluation they can. This assessment will be written and shared with the person evaluated and others involved in the assessment system. The results lead to other decisions, plans, and goals. It is important for you to document your findings often in the ongoing evaluative process. Rarely does anyone complain when final scores or comments are excellent, but still, your rationale for the judgment provides validity. Practically speaking, it will help you write a better evaluation because you will be able to supply supporting detail. When evaluating a student teacher who will be receiving average or less than satisfactory comments or scores, the presence of documentation is even more important. (Chapter 9 will assist you in working with mentees who are struggling.)

Let us now take a closer look at the evaluation process we recommend that you follow for success with your new-teacher partner. You will draw on all of the resources you have available both to support your mentee (in your role as coach) and to provide honest, accurate feedback and assessment (in your role as evaluator).

HOW THE PROCESS CAN WORK FOR YOU

Responsibility for evaluation of preservice and new teachers rarely falls exclusively on the shoulders of mentors, and it is important for you and your partner to understand how the system functions. Your district has procedures established for supervision and evaluation. Some procedures, often specifying time lines and data sources, may be dictated by state law or negotiated agreement (Danielson, 1996). Danielson and McGreal (2000) believe that a supervision process for new teachers should involve adequate time and effort on the part of the evaluators, multiple participants, and use of primary sources of data. There must also be in place procedures to ensure equity and protection of due process. In what we believe to be the best models of supervision, teachers play an important professional and collegial role in their own evaluation. Carr and Harris (2001) suggest that supervision should follow four steps: self-assessment, goal setting, colleague consultation, and summative evaluation. We value the inclusion of the teacher in reflection, goal setting, and consultation elements of the process. In most districts, mentors as support providers may have the opportunity to use many communication, observation, feedback, and assessment processes to help their mentees succeed during the first year.

Cooperating teachers have a clear role in evaluation because they nearly always complete a final summative evaluation. In the teacher education program, preservice teachers are likely to have completed and been evaluated in several field experiences. At multiple checkpoints, they will have been assessed and judged able to move to the next stage. If their program adheres to high standards, they also will have completed many reflective and self-evaluative exercises. The multiple evaluations are designed to ensure that competent (or better) student teachers enter student teaching and that competent (or better) beginning teachers are recommended for teacher licensure. The cooperating teacher's summative evaluation can have a critical effect on the final outcome of a preservice teacher's program.

Preparing the Summative Evaluation

Preparing the summative evaluation should start at the beginning of the field experience, not the end. Early in the experience, you should develop an understanding of the goals for student teaching as described on the summative evaluation form provided by the partner university. Exercise 8.2 lists questions for you to ask to understand your expectations and those of your mentee. Based on answers to these questions and others you may formulate, you will work with the student teacher to set goals, to schedule learning and teaching experiences, and to collect and analyze appropriate data.

Your final judgment will be shared in a written report on the university's standard form. The form may require scaled ratings and/or narrative summaries of performance according to the institution's standards. Table 8.5 shows a sample narrative summative evaluation. The form, based on the student teaching evaluation form used at California State University, Fullerton (2002), includes categories that show a strong link to the standards of NBPTS. The evaluator uses the space provided to give clear and specific comments describing performance in each standard. Individual strengths and goal areas in important teaching elements can be described. This type of form relies not only on the evaluator's judgment but also in part on the evaluator's writing skill. It is time consuming to do a thorough and accurate narrative assessment but, done well, it can provide useful and substantive information.

A sample form that uses a combined rating scale and narrative summary, based on the student teaching evaluation at the University of Minnesota, Morris, (University of Minnesota-Morris Teacher Education, 2002), is shown in Form 8.1. On this form, the evaluator rates the candidate on ten program standards—in this case based on INTASC standards—and then provides a summary statement. This form allows the rater both to provide a brief assessment on ten important teaching elements and also to provide examples and support in narrative form. The ratings assigned in that portion of the evaluation are of course susceptible to the validity and reliability errors discussed earlier. Whatever form the evaluation takes, adherence to rigorous standards of fairness and accuracy is necessary.

Even when all of the assessment procedures are followed exactly, it is difficult sometimes to write the summative evaluation, especially if low ratings or negative comments are needed. However, this task can also be troubling when judgments between *good* comments and *excellent* ones are called for. One cooperating teacher shares her experience:

> In the section where you write comments, I was very honest about giving high marks on some things . . . but reflecting honestly on others where it hadn't progressed the way it should. When I wrote the commentary, I never wrote anything like "I without hesitation would recommend this person to be hired." I didn't say not to hire her, but I didn't put any general recommendation. It was difficult because I've been on hiring committees,

(Text continued on page 128)

Table 8.5 Sample Narrative Summative Evaluation Form

Creating and Maintaining an Effective Environment for Student Learning	Understanding and Organizing Subject Matter for Student Learning
Planning Instruction and Designing Learning Experiences for All Students	Engaging and Supporting All Students in Learning
Assessing Student Learning	Developing as a Professional Educator

SOURCE: Adapted from California State University, Fullerton (2002)

Form 8.1   Sample Summative Evaluation With Rating Scale

Please circle the numbers that most accurately describe the above candidate's performance in each category. In the space provided, comment on the qualifications of this candidate as a prospective teacher. This form will become part of the candidate's permanent file.

(1 = Unsatisfactory, 2 = Below Average, 3 = Average, 4 = Above Average, 5 = Outstanding)

Knowledge of Subject Matter	1	2	3	4	5
Student Learning	1	2	3	4	5
Diverse Learners	1	2	3	4	5
Instructional Strategies	1	2	3	4	5
Learning Environment/Classroom Management	1	2	3	4	5
Communication	1	2	3	4	5
Planning Instruction	1	2	3	4	5
Assessment	1	2	3	4	5
Reflection & Professional Development	1	2	3	4	5
Collaboration, Ethics, & Relationships	1	2	3	4	5

Comments:

Signature _____ Professional Title _____ Date _____

Address _____

_____

_____ Telephone _____

SOURCE: Adapted from University of Minnesota-Morris Teacher Education (2002)

and you hire someone who had great recommendations and then find out they're not so good. I couldn't ethically say something that wasn't true. I accurately described what I saw.

Supervisors in general are more comfortable coaching and providing feedback than they are completing summative evaluations. However, it is our professional responsibility as teacher educators to complete the written record of performance.

Communicating Results

You and your mentee should talk early and often about the summative evaluation. Dialogue focused on goals is a powerful way to help both mentee and mentor to learn about classroom practice and to support growth. Both of you should be collecting data and analyzing it in terms of common standards you set early in your relationship. The process should provide rich opportunities for self-assessment and professional discussions.

"Imagination gallops; judgment merely walks."

—Traditional proverb
(quoted in Creative Quotations, 2002)

Even if the university does not require a mid-term evaluation, we strongly suggest that you, your student teacher, and possibly the university supervisor create one. New teacher partners want to know how they are doing, and they should never be surprised. Here are sample comments that show their need for ongoing feedback:

- "Don't fall behind on evaluations. Hold the student teacher accountable. Give advice, ideas, share units. All of this helps."
- "There was a discrepancy between my formative evals and summative eval. I would like to have known more about my weaknesses or areas of improvement before the summative so I could adjust and show growth."

You can easily use the summative evaluation form midway through the experience to discuss perceptions and assessments of progress. Think about how you would assess the student teacher if you were expected to complete the summative evaluation at that point. Have the student teacher do the same. Compare the two evaluations and the reasons for your judgments. If everything is going well, you can set even higher goals for achievement. If there are areas for improvement, work with the student teacher to set goals. In most cases, you will be working to help a student teacher shift from adequate to good performance or from good to excellent. Rarely, you will be working with a student teacher who is struggling with serious problems. Chapter 9 will help you prepare for that situation.

At the end of the experience, after completing the summative evaluation, supervisors should share their assessments. If you've done the legwork, there will be few surprises for the student teacher. Use the final conference as a time to set future goals. It is often a time for celebration, congratulations, and best wishes. Be aware however, that when you discover what elements of your summative evaluation surprise your mentee, you may be surprised! Some cooperating teachers have called us in dismay when a student teacher has argued about a good comment that apparently was not good enough! Time, kindness, patience, communication—and data—will help you to help your mentee understand. We hope that the exercises that follow will help you in this important task.

EXERCISES

Exercise 8.1   The Top Five Skills for Beginning Teachers

Determine what *you* believe to be essential skills for beginning teachers.

1. Complete the chart by listing the top five skills you believe your student teacher should have mastered at the end of the student teaching experience. Then, try to fill in descriptors to create a simple evaluation rubric.
2. How did your top five compare to the sample evaluations in the chapter?
3. Make a copy of the completed chart for your student teacher to complete. How do the two charts compare? Have your principal complete the chart and compare it to your chart and that of your student teacher.
4. How would you rate yourself on the chart? What elements were hardest for you when you first began teaching? What specific things can you do to help your student teacher attain high marks on your top five?

Top Five Skills for Beginning Teachers

Skill Area	Low	Satisfactory	Target
1.			
2.			
3.			
4.			
5.			
Sample: Gets along with school staff.	Often makes demands rather than requests; shows ingratitude or disrespect; makes little effort to get to know support staff.	Understands roles and responsibilities; addresses them professionally.	Includes support staff as important members of the learning process; treats them respectfully and appropriately.

Exercise 8.2   Summative Evaluation: Questions to Ask and Answer

Early in the experience, you need to study the format of the summative evaluation you will be expected to complete. Be sure that you have answers to the following questions and any others you may have. Program materials often contain valuable information. Program directors or university supervisors will assist you as well. Be sure to understand your expected role as evaluator and the processes you will need to follow.

Questions	Answers
Do all categories or elements of the form align with formative evaluation materials and processes? If not, how will you build them into your formative assessments?	
If applicable, what are scoring criteria? (For example, what makes an "excellent" an "excellent?")	
What documentation might be used to support each category of assessment?	
Who will be the audience for the completed form?	
Who will write the final draft of the evaluation? Is the form available electronically? Is there secretarial support to prepare a final copy?	
To what extent are your top five skills for beginning teachers represented on the summative evaluation form?	
What evidence is there that the form is a valid measurement of good teaching?	

Exercise 8.3   Measuring Up to the Role of Evaluator

The following criteria are drawn from "Guiding Principles for Evaluators," prepared by an American Evaluation Association (AEA) task force (1994). The principles are designed for professional evaluators, but we find them relevant to your work as mentors. Based on your reading of the chapter, describe key actions that you would take to meet the guidelines. Then, visit the AEA Web site (at www.eval.org/EvaluationDocuments/aeaprin6.html) to compare their explanations to the ones you devised. Which ones will be growth areas for you?

Evaluators Will:	My Explanation	AEA Description
1. Carry out systematic, data-based assessment		
2. Perform competently		
3. Demonstrate honesty and integrity		
4. Respect the security, dignity, and self-worth of those they evaluate.		
5. Consider diverse interests and values related to the general and public welfare.		

SOURCE: Drawn from American Evaluation Association (AEA) task force (1994)

Exercise 8.4   Evaluating Evaluation

Establish reliability by comparing your assessments with those of knowledgeable others. Here are methods for formative and summative evaluation:

1. Have your new teacher partner complete a lesson self-evaluation for a lesson that you observed. Compare findings. Discuss criteria and reasons for your decisions.

2. Observe the same lesson that the university supervisor observes. Complete the standard observation form. Compare findings. Discuss criteria and reasons for your decisions.

3. Observe a videotaped lesson with other cooperating teachers, the university supervisor, or the principal. Assess the lesson; share and compare findings. Discuss criteria and reasons for your decision.

4. Complete a draft of the summative evaluation several weeks before the end of the field experience. Compare assessments with the university supervisor or other evaluators. If ratings are used, look to see if scores vary more than one increment (e.g., a score of 5 by one evaluator and a score of 3 by another). If the assessment is in narrative form, look to see if the overall tone and findings are consistent. Discuss criteria and rationale for your decisions.

9

Working With a Teacher in Trouble

It was just really difficult. . . . You want so badly for this person to come in and be a good teacher and to feel like you've sent someone really good off into the profession who has a little bit of you. . . . It was difficult not to be successful . . . and to write that final recommendation with comments that weren't very good.

My principal asked me, "Can he teach? Would his students learn? Could I really recommend him?" Of course, the answer was "No."

—A cooperating teacher

Though all student teachers face some difficulties during student teaching (and all beginning teachers face difficulties during their first years in their own classrooms), only a very few fit the category of *teacher in trouble*. You have read and thought about the intricacies of building relationships with novice teachers, supporting their growth, providing guidance and instruction, and making final evaluations. It can be hard work, and in the *vast majority* of cases, the effort is worthwhile. To see a new teacher blossom in skill and confidence and to know you were a part of it is a glorious experience. We wish that experience for all of our readers. What happens, however, when efforts do not result in blossoming skill and confidence? What happens when your new teacher partner is in real trouble? What are the appropriate procedures that must be implemented to provide the accuracy, sensitivity, professionalism, and decision making that ensure that students will have qualified teachers who at the very least meet minimum standards? Reflect upon those questions as you meet Rhonda and Karl, two struggling beginners.

Note to Support Providers

In many states, people who mentor newly credentialed teachers through an induction program do not serve as gatekeepers. That is, they have no formal summative evaluation role or power to remove a troubled teacher from the classroom. That presents a different set of rules and demands for working with a teacher in trouble. If you are a support provider in a similar position, you can follow many of the same strategies suggested in this chapter for student teachers. Some of these tips may prove helpful as well:

1. Talk with program leaders to clarify your role and the range of possible actions you can take.

2. Double-check confidentiality requirements. What information regarding classroom performance are you allowed to share with program leaders, site administrators, or other relevant parties? Respect the boundaries of confidentiality.

3. Talk with your new teacher partner and build a large support team that can provide assistance. Program leaders should be able to help. Enlist them early.

4. After you are clear on the extent of your role, work fully within that capacity and let go of issues that are outside your circle of influence. Provide the most humane and caring support you can to foster your partner's satisfaction and protect quality of classroom life for the students involved. Remember to display faith and public regard for your partner's strengths and areas of competence.

5. Think about nondirective, collaborative, and directive approaches to support (Chapter 6). You may need to vary your level of intervention. Allow your partner to maintain the highest level of autonomy possible.

6. Listen actively as your new teacher wrestles with intense issues of potential professional and personal failure. Respect your partner's competence as an adult, even if your partner is working outside the range of his or her expertise by teaching.

WHAT WOULD YOU DO?

Rhonda is a loner. In her first year of teaching, she has connected very little with the other high school English teachers. Keeping to herself, she neither seeks nor appreciates advice or hints from others. Her principal has observed her three times and has expressed concern about her lack of creativity and control, as well as her overt criticism of others. Rhonda's school district has a new-teacher mentoring program, and her assigned mentor, an experienced and respected member of the English faculty, also worries about Rhonda's performance. The mentor has tried to discuss curriculum, planning, and expected programming with Rhonda but has reported to the director of the program that communication is not going well. "Rhonda is smart enough, but she doesn't put in the time. I have scheduled meetings with her that she cancels at the last minute. I have made suggestions that she hasn't tried. Her students are rude and disrespectful. She is either sarcastic to them or oblivious to what they're saying. I don't see much learning going on. I wonder if the problem is that she doesn't like me. I would be happy to let her work with another mentor, but she hasn't connected with anyone else, either."

Karl has completed about ten weeks of his fifteen-week full-time student teaching. Everything about him is big: his size, his dreams, and his booming voice. Prior to student teaching he had received average or above-average evaluations from practicum supervisors. During the summers, he had enjoyed working as a camp counselor, and the camp director recommended him for the elementary teaching program. Problems in student teaching, however, surfaced immediately. Though he writes detailed plans, he seems unable to implement them. In front of the students, he seems confused. In response to the students' disrespectful behavior during his lessons, he has begun yelling at them. His university supervisor, who spotted the problem immediately, has met with him regularly. After five weeks, the cooperating teacher and university supervisor met with Karl to make their concerns explicit. They described their observations of the problems he was having with instruction, relationship with students, and his classroom management. They expressed their concern about his well-being. Though admitting that he sometimes cried when he thought about how poorly things were going, he said, "But I know I can be a good teacher." Together, the three made a plan for improvement. But five weeks later, the problems are worsening. The cooperating teacher remarked to the university supervisor, "Even though I am worried about the kids and getting calls from parents, I keep thinking about Karl. He wants to be a teacher so badly. But he is disintegrating. Everybody is. I feel like a failure."

Take a moment to consider how you would answer these questions if you were mentoring Rhonda or Karl:

- What would be your biggest concern?
- What would be the best plan of action?
- What would you need to know?
- Who would you like to help you?

Your thoughts about these questions undoubtedly reveal the complexity and challenge of helping someone struggle in his or her growth toward becoming a teacher. In no situation more than this one are your dual roles of supporter and evaluator more at odds. As a teacher educator, you are compelled to support your new teacher partner's learning. You are also compelled to uphold the standards of our profession. Thus you are called to be both advocate and gatekeeper (Page, Rudney, & Marxen, 2002). This chapter offers recommendations and support to those who may confront what is potentially the most difficult and disturbing obligation of a cooperating teacher or mentor. We explore the questions that should frame your analysis, outline a general procedure for creating and evaluating improvement plans, and suggest ways to assist your new teacher partner through difficult times.

FRAMING THE STRUGGLE

> "Happy families are all alike; every unhappy family is unhappy in its own way."
>
> —Leo Tolstoy, *Anna Karenina*
> (quoted in An Online Library of Literature, 2002; original work published in 1875)

You have already read earlier in this book about guiding your partner and executing a coherent, comprehensive assessment process for him or her. You know, then, about focusing on patterns of behavior in multiple areas. You understand the importance of forming judgments based on the data you have collected. Usually, your observations and assessments indicate that your mentee is at the very least making reasonable progress and exhibiting an expected pattern of growth and performance. If your observations, experiences, and data have created doubts in your mind about your student teacher's competence, your student teacher has real trouble, and you have decisions to make and actions take. Before you jump into action, think carefully about what your data tell you.

The next three sections include questions you should ask to help you interpret your data. Because the concepts are interconnected, thinking about one question will assist you in thinking about another. No matter what the answers, work will need to be done.

Lack of Probable Potential or Presence of Developmental Delay?

> "Apparent failure may hold in its rough shell the germs of a success that will blossom in time, and bear fruit throughout eternity."
>
> —Frances Watkins Harper
> (quoted in Creative Quotations, 2002)

The very first thing you need to think about is whether your new teacher partner has the potential to learn and become a good teacher. You have read about teacher development and the typical pattern of growth. Is your student teacher not growing at all, or is his or her progress alarmingly slow? We have seen student teachers who ultimately succeeded though there were moments of doubt for the cooperating teachers, university supervisors, and sometimes the student teachers themselves. They may have started with a deficit in skill, knowledge, or disposition that they had to surmount. Imagine, for example, a student teacher who has limited subject-matter knowledge in many areas. She realizes she is behind her peers and becomes defensive. When planning, she avoids difficult subject matter and delivers superficial and trite instruction. She comforts herself with the notion that she is a good person and cares about her students. She focuses on her belief that what matters is that students learn how to learn. She reminds herself that she had really smart teachers who did not teach her a thing. She still identifies most closely with the student role, as in a very early stage of teacher development (Fuller & Bown, 1975). If this habit of mind and action is pervasive and immutable, this student teacher may indeed lack the potential to improve. However, if, in your careful analysis, you recognize the source of her trouble and see possible corrective measures, you may be able to help her grow. There are actions she can take to improve, and your data may suggest she will be able—with support, structure, and encouragements—to make necessary adjustments.

Your careful analysis might instead lead you to doubt probable potential for success. Though we have seen some student teachers manage to overcome difficulties, we also have seen others fail. A charming, young student teacher relies on personality to conceal poor professional decisions and performance. He is consistently late, ill prepared, and ineffective. At first his supervisors believe that he has not had time to understand expectations. But with time, suggestions, guidance, support, and explanations, there still is no sign of improvement. If the *pattern* of behavior fails to improve or worsens, we may infer a lack of probable potential for success. Sometimes in cases such as these, you will hear people remark, "I'm so disappointed in my student teacher. He has such potential but wastes it." Though we understand the meaning behind those words, we offer this alternative, "My student teacher is personable, but he does not have the probable potential to meet the requirements for teacher licensure."

Lack of Ability or Lack of Teachability?

You have explored the notion of teaching ability throughout this book and certainly throughout your own teacher preparation and career. Licensure and National Board standards, professional development programs, and your principal's lesson observations explain or imply what teachers ought to do.

> A man can fail many times, but he isn't a failure until he begins to blame somebody else.
>
> —John Burroughs (also attributed to J. Paul Getty) (quoted in Creative Quotations, 2002)

When mentoring a struggling novice teacher, you must consider whether he or she has the *ability* to meet accepted standards for teaching. Is there sufficient knowledge or ability to learn? Can your student teacher communicate effectively with others? Can he or she plan, implement, and assess lessons that result in meaningful student learning? *Teachability* is a disposition held by a person who is willing to consider and act upon suggestions from knowledgeable others, reflect on practice, and commit to continuous learning (Page et al., 2002). Those with low teachability seem to disregard—or to react defensively—to suggestions and concerns of others. They often have an external locus of control, where problems encountered in the classroom are attributed to causes outside of their own actions. They might say, "Nobody told me I would have to . . . . The mentor teacher didn't let me . . . . The students are unmotivated." In other words, they blame others for their own troubles. Preservice or beginning teachers who are *teachable* progress more rapidly and achieve more success than those less open to the guidance of others.

Differences in teachability and ability, as shown in Table 9.1, combine to create distinct learning characteristics and thus point to different coaching actions (Page et al., 2002). A teaching partner in any of the three quadrants in Table 9.1 could very well be struggling. (If your mentee is of high ability and highly teachable, the quadrant not shown in this table, he or she is not the topic of this chapter!)

Marginal or Failing Performance?

Would I want this person to teach my children? Almost as part of professional folklore, people often say that the answer to that question is how they judge a student teacher's success. If only we could actually use such a litmus test. You and I

Table 9.1   Supervisory Behaviors According to Candidate Ability and Teachability

Candidate Characteristics	Supervisor Behaviors	
	Advocacy	Gatekeeping
Ability: Low Teachability: Low	Devote substantial time to continuous encouragement and critical, specific feedback	Clarify and enforce programmatic expectations; implement learning plans and probationary procedures; counsel candidates into other areas of study
Ability: Low Teachability: High	Provide academic assistance, encouragement, and specific feedback	Monitor academic progress and implement programmatic checkpoints and benchmarks
Ability: High Teachability: Low	Stress reflection on professionalism and taking on the role of teacher	Clarify and enforce programmatic expectations; implement learning plans and probationary procedures

SOURCE: Drawn from the work of Page, Rudney, and Marxen (2002)

and almost everyone else want only the very best for our children. If only the very best were licensed, hired, and tenured, what a wonderful world this would be. Unfortunately, not everyone can be the very best. When it comes to the high-stakes decision about whether or not to recommend candidates for teaching licensure, we are bound by the established levels of minimum competency. We have standards that say to us, here are the *minimum* skills, knowledge, and dispositions that every beginning teacher must have. All who meet minimum standards will be recommended. Luckily, minimum standards are reasonably high, and most candidates have a collection of skills, experiences, and attitudes that makes them rise far above minimum levels. Most of our candidates exceed the minimum, and that is good for us all. Still, if your teacher partner is facing a serious struggle, you may have to decide not *how* but *if* a candidate will become a teacher. Sometimes a student teacher must be removed from student teaching because of failure to meet successfully the demands and requirements of teaching. It is incredibly difficult to make such a decision. It is equally difficult to watch someone who manages to meet minimum competencies, but at barely acceptable levels.

We see three categories of "marginal" performance:

- *People not suited for the profession.* With sensitive assistance from cooperating teachers or supervisors and often on their own, these candidates recognize the mismatch between a career in teaching and their true interests and skills. They are able to choose a career more suited to their strengths and abilities.

- *People whose skills are fragile and very dependent upon a particular context.* They may, for example, do very well with young students but founder with older. They may thrive in a very structured environment but struggle if expected to function in alternative settings (e.g., an open classroom or block scheduling).

- *People who cannot see their lack of aptitude and do not make improvements.* They believe their performance is not so bad and is a result of factors outside their control. These are the most difficult to assist because their view of reality is so different from the view of those around them—and those around them are in charge of evaluating them.

Now What?

After a thoughtful analysis of your mentee's struggle, you may be discouraged. As we explained, any answers to the questions in the preceding sections will require hard work. Supervisors need to spend time and energy to help a person who is having serious difficulties either succeed, decide to withdraw, or accept their failure with as much dignity as possible. The next section will help you to create an action plan.

HELPING YOUR MENTEE UNDERSTAND THE PROBLEM

Student teachers with serious problems need time, support, and clear communication. Criticisms must be made in a manner that allows the student teacher to take ownership of the problem and gives them sufficient time to explore and practice corrective strategies. Box 9.1 offers typical steps to follow in the formal process of guiding and assessing a student teacher in trouble. It is important to involve the university supervisor or liaison

> "Keep on beginning and failing. Each time you fail, start all over again, and you will grow stronger until you have accomplished a purpose—not the one you began with perhaps, but one you'll be glad to remember."
>
> —Anne Sullivan
> (quoted in Creative Quotations, 2002)

early in the process. A team approach to resolving serious difficulties in student teaching is the best approach (Weaver & Stanulis, 1996; Zheng & Webb, 2000). The cooperating teacher, university supervisor or liaison, and the student teacher must all be involved in communicating concerns and working to address them as soon as possible. Often the school principal has information and support to provide. Others may also be important to this evaluation support team. If the situation is serious, we encourage the student teacher to bring an advocate—someone who will help not only clarify the student teacher's position but help him or her to understand perspectives of others. Including knowledgeable people in the process will introduce new ideas and potential solutions, increase validity, and help assure that final decisions are fair and supportable. Be sure to refer to university or district guidelines concerning *legal* advocates. If the mentee brings legal counsel, the evaluation team might need to include its own legal advisor.

Box 9.1   Formal Communication of Concerns: Suggested Steps

---

1. Analyze observation and anecdotal data to ascertain specific concerns and problem areas.

2. Discuss concerns with university supervisor or liaison.

3. Communicate concerns in writing (see Exercise 9.2 for ideas). Include description of previous corrective efforts.

4. Schedule a meeting with student teacher, university liaison, and other members of the evaluation team. Inform the student teacher that he or she may invite an advocate.

5. At the meeting, design a plan for improvement that includes specific steps, evaluation procedures, and time line (see Exercise 9.3 for ideas).

6. Assist the student teacher in plan implementation and assessment.

7. With evaluation team members, completely analyze progress.

8. Use assessment data to recommend continuation in program (perhaps with extended improvement plan) or withdrawal from program.

9. With university supervisor, communicate decision to student teacher.

Danielson and McGreal (2000) describe support and evaluation procedures for *tenured* teachers who have been identified as marginal teachers—"those who, in the professional judgment of an administrator, are experiencing difficulty in meeting one or more of the district's standards for effective teaching" (p. 118). Their three phases are designed for teacher awareness, assistance, and disciplinary action. We draw on their model and suggest a general procedure to work with preservice or beginning teachers who are experiencing major difficulties in meeting relevant professional standards. In the three-phase process described here, evaluators build awareness, provide specific assistance, and make final decisions.

Awareness Phase

Usually, though not always, the beginner is aware of the serious difficulties he or she is experiencing. Having followed proper supervision procedures, you have conducted frequent observation and provided substantial feedback. When unusual problems exist, it is necessary to hold a conference with your partner and the university supervisor to make the student teacher aware that the problems are serious and might affect his or her continuation in the program or recommendation for licensure. In this phase, it is important to communicate the concerns in writing, prepare documentation, and hold a conference with the student teacher and members of the evaluation team. The exercises in this chapter are designed to help you prepare for your meeting with your student teacher and represent a sample of the sort of materials your university may provide for you. Comments from student teachers

---

Box 9.2   Words From Student Teachers Who Struggled and Succeeded

---

"She pushed me! I would begin to get better in an area, and she stretched me to be even stronger. She had very high expectations for me as a person and also as a teacher. This was the biggest help."

"She didn't put me down; she was always very positive, and that built my confidence. She shared experiences from her teaching, and it helped me see that everyone makes mistakes, and you learn and grow from them."

"Keep a tighter reign on your student teacher in the beginning."

---

and cooperating teachers in Box 9.2 attest to the importance of communicating high expectations and support.

The conference itself can be quite difficult. As seasoned teachers, you have had to do this before when giving bad news to your students or their parents. Those experiences tell you that the results are going to be unpredictable and depend very much on the combination of interactions, personalities, and events that form the history of your relationship with the student teacher. Depending on the role you play within the university's teacher education program, you or the university supervisor may lead the conference. Whether or not you are leading the conference, what you say matters a great deal to your partner. Student teachers are most receptive to constructive criticism, especially of a serious nature, when the critic is also someone they see as their advocate (Page et al., 2002). You are likely to be that person in your student teacher's eyes. As a beginning teacher, one of the authors learned of F. Wunderman's suggestions for successful conferences. Adapted below for use with a struggling mentee, these suggestions can help you communicate sensitively:

- *Be honest.* You have collected the data and checked with others to see that it is accurate. In clear, simple language, state the problem as you see it. Be kind, but tell the truth.

- *Be accepting.* Your student teacher will react to the news, and many reactions are possible. We have seen tears, anger, and defensiveness. We have also seen resignation, discouragement, and grim acceptance. And we have seen relief, gratitude, and hope. Whatever comes your way—short of true threat—be accepting of your student teacher's feelings. Listen and take notes. Useful information may come from statements of feeling.

- *Be patient.* It may take time for teachers in trouble to understand fully the nature of the problem and the seriousness of the situation. They may have trouble understanding the corrective behaviors expected. They may need to hear information more than once. Be patient with yourself as well. Give yourself some time to adapt to a difficult situation.

- *Be professional.* Prior to reaching the decision to have a conference such as this, you will have exercised your best professional skill in observation, feedback, analysis, and decision making. During the conference, you will need to remain calm, kind, and assertive. Honest statements of your frustrations are acceptable. Angry or defensive remarks are not. Remember that the goal of the conference is to help the student teacher toward success in one form or another.

• *Be yourself.* Retaining some sense of normalcy will help diffuse tension. Be all the things listed here, but embody them in a way that will make sense to you and your mentee.

Assistance Phase

If building awareness is successful, the student teacher and his or her mentors have a clear list of things to do. For each major concern, there is a set of tasks or behaviors that will address it. The evaluation support team has established criteria and time line for satisfactory achievement of goals, determined methods of documentation, and chosen the people who will be completing the assessment. The plans are set, but now the work (yes, more work!) must be done. You have read throughout the book about three things that student teachers and beginning teachers need: faith, freedom, and feedback. These three ideas will help you work during the assistance phase, when your mentee is attempting to build skills and needs much support.

Though you as cooperating teachers may not be convinced your mentees will succeed, you are hopeful that they will, are willing to let them try, and are ready to invest time and effort to support them. That's *faith*. Encourage them to do their best. Continue to model professional behaviors and clarify expectations. Continue to teach them. Mentors, you may not be convinced your mentees can make it on their own, but you are willing to let them try. That is giving them *freedom*. Step back and let student teachers meet the expectations. Provide support but don't "save" them. At the end of this phase, the evaluation team will know whether or not your partner has met the stated goals at a satisfactory level. You will have continued to observe, reflect, and share your findings. That's *feedback*. Review performance on the predetermined assessment measures frequently so that there are no surprises.

Making Final Decisions

Based on the data collected during the probationary phase, members of the evaluation team—along with the student teacher—will decide what will happen in terms of program continuance or completion. There are numerous possibilities, but here are the four most likely to occur based on our experience:

• *The student teacher succeeds.* This result is the one we strive for, and it is usually a welcome one. Sometimes the student teacher needed an extra boost (or what one of our success stories called "a kick in the pants"). When a candidate meets only minimum standards, the result is not wholly satisfying. As mentioned earlier, we want only the very best teachers in our profession. Part of your professional responsibility is to complete a final evaluation of your student teacher. The language you use in your narrative summaries or the ratings you give on the university's forms will allow you to describe accurately the student teacher's achievement. It is up to the districts that hire "marginal" performers to support their continued development. You have done your job.

• *The student teacher is given more time.* Proponents of mastery learning believe that instead of holding time constant and allowing achievement levels to vary, teachers should allow more time to some students so that maximum learning can be achieved by all (see Good & Brophy, 1994, for a description of mastery learning). Sometimes for student teachers, giving more time does indeed increase their achievement. If the objectives are not met by the due date, but the cooperating teachers and university supervisors are encouraged by a pattern of improvement, and resources are available, the probationary period can be extended or additional student teaching time can be required. If time is extended, new goals, tasks, criteria, and schedule should be established.

• *The student teacher withdraws.* Sometimes this is the most happily received result. On his or her own, or with counseling from mentors and others, a student teacher may come to realize that teaching is not the right profession. A disappointment, perhaps, but the decision usually brings great relief to all of those involved in the process.

• *The student teacher is withdrawn.* When the student teacher fails to meet the objectives and shows no probability of satisfactory improvement, he or she will be withdrawn from the program. Who takes the final action to withdraw a student teacher depends upon the established roles and guidelines in the specific teacher education program. In the traditional supervision model, the university supervisor or other representative will be responsible for explaining the decision and assisting the student in exiting procedures. Even in models where cooperating teachers hold primary responsibility for all student teacher evaluations and decision making, they can expect support and guidance from the university.

SUCCESSFUL RESOLUTION

Although you are vitally interested in your student teacher's success, your first allegiance must be to the students and to the profession. Therefore, the notion of success must be reinterpreted. Any one of the results described above can be deemed a *success* if it accurately reflects the performance, probable potential, and professionalism of the student teacher affected. As you work with your student teacher to resolve difficulties, keep this question in the back of your mind: Is this person suitable for working with children and adolescents as a credentialed teacher? Your "yes" or "no" answer to this question, along with the qualifiers and explanations you can provide, must guide your actions and decisions. We hope that you never need the information in this chapter but that, if you do, you find it helpful.

EXERCISES

Exercise 9.1   Framing the Struggle

Complete the chart to identify the nature of the problem with a struggling novice. You can practice by choosing Karl or Rhonda using the sketchy information provided in the case studies earlier in this chapter. You can also choose your own student teacher or another teacher you know who may be having problems. A review of Chapters 7 and 8 may assist you in gathering supporting evidence.

Questions	Answers
Is there a delay in the professional development? What is the evidence?	
Is there evidence that suggests potential for success? How likely is success?	
In what elements of teaching does the teacher partner show ability? Are there areas of deficiency?	
How teachable is the teacher partner? How have suggestions been received and enacted?	
If the judgment had to be made today, would I say that this novice had met *minimum* competency in all areas?	
In what areas has the beginner exceeded minimum competency?	
What areas of strength are so excellent that I can accept marginal competence in others?	
In what areas has the candidate failed to meet minimum standards?	

Exercise 9.2   Communication of Concern

Prospective teachers must fulfill the expectations of professional educators. When these expectations are not met, and if a pattern of behavior continues after discussion with the student teacher, formal corrective measures are necessary. Please use this form (or one provided by your university) to communicate serious concerns to your student teacher and to the university liaison. This form is adapted from the Teacher Education Program at the University of Minnesota-Morris (University of Minnesota-Morris Teacher Education, 2002). It is a first step prior to establishing a formal improvement plan.

Candidate Name _____

Current Course or Field Experience _____

Date _____

1. **Indicate below specific concerns about the professional actions of this student teacher.**

   The student teacher demonstrates difficulty in the following areas:
   - ☐ Taking responsibility for own actions
   - ☐ Seeking help when needed
   - ☐ Considering and utilizing suggestions and reflective feedback
   - ☐ Striving for quality and completeness
   - ☐ Managing time well
   - ☐ Arriving on time and preparing for the day
   - ☐ Generating and submitting work in a timely fashion
   - ☐ Collaborating
   - ☐ Demonstrating respect for others
   - ☐ Demonstrating sensitivity or responsiveness to students
   - ☐ Using resources and materials appropriately
   - ☐ Designing and acting on goals and plans
   - ☐ Demonstrating academic and professional integrity
   - ☐ Taking responsibility for the safety and welfare of students
   - ☐ Maintaining a drug-free work environment
   - ☐ Other: _____

2. **Briefly explain your reason(s) for concern.**

3. **Describe previous efforts to communicate concerns or provide assistance.**

Your Name and Title _____   **Your Signature**_____

SOURCE: Adapted from University of Minnesota-Morris Teacher Education (2002)

Exercise 9.3 Early Interventions

Early identification of problems provides time for early corrective measures. Here is a list of interventions that experienced cooperating teachers and supervisors have used successfully to resolve difficulties for student teachers. Select the most relevant ones to try and record the results. Please let us know if they were helpful and send us your own ideas.

Interventions to Try	Results
Increase communication with university supervisor. Ask for an early triad conference to clarify expectations.	
Review handbook with the student teacher.	
Give direct instruction in problem areas (e.g., teaching strategies or classroom management). Present ideas to try, check for the student teacher's understanding, and guide his or her practice of the new technique. A student teacher in trouble may not be able to infer good practice just through observation.	
Partner-teach lessons in trouble areas. Plan and implement the lessons together.	
Alternate teaching with your student teacher every other day. This allows your student teacher to see you model good teaching and allows you to protect student learning.	
Request detailed plans for every lesson in advance. Have the student teacher explain each step to you. Provide student teacher with a write-up of required changes as well as suggestions.	
Give *written* feedback daily. Keep copies.	
Create a checklist of the things you expect to see. Allow the student teacher to review and adapt the list. Use the checklist daily.	
Keep documentation of observations and anecdotes. Journals, notes on your plan book, and 3"-by-5" cards are useful.	
Discuss discipline problems. Ask for reflection. Encourage the student teacher to try a variety of strategies.	
Others?	

Exercise 9.4   Preparing for a Difficult Conference

Collect your thoughts and your data prior to meeting with a struggling new-teacher partner. The following table will help you organize your thoughts and evidence.

Key Points	Evidence	Minimum Expectations	Questions to Ask
Example: Often tardy and unprepared	• Arrival times listed in plan book • Lesson samples • Anecdotal records • Dates of meetings where expectations were discussed	1. In classroom by 7:30 a.m. every morning. 2. Present in classroom prior to each class period starting. 3. Lesson plans and materials ready the day before teaching.	1. What adjustments can you make to your schedule so that you can arrive on time? 2. When do you typically do your planning? 3. How can I help you in your lesson preparation?

Exercise 9.5   Conference Format

Use or adapt this format to assist you in holding a meaningful, productive conference. Take notes on the conference sheet to document the process. (An example of a completed form follows the blank form.)

Date: _____ Time: _____ Location: _____
People Present: _____

A. *Opening*: Remember to establish a professional and caring tone. Be honest and kind.

　　1. *Introductions if necessary*: Be sure that everyone present knows the others in attendance.

　　2. *Purpose of the conference*: State in clear terms. Prepare in advance.

　　3. *Context statement*: Recognize the complexity of the situation, the student teacher's strength areas, and his or her efforts. Honestly express concern.

B. *Communication of concern*: Be specific.

　　1. *Overview of concerns*: Briefly explain the concerns you will discuss. Select only those that are most important and that must be corrected.

　　2. *Specific concerns*: For each concern, explicitly describe the problem. Give examples. Show documentation. Explain why it matters. Check for understanding and solicit input. Listen to the student teacher's questions and concerns. Keeping a chart such as the following might be helpful.

Explain Concern	Check for Understanding	Student Teacher's Questions and Concerns

C. *Plan for improvement:* Discuss ways to address and assess concerns. The team completes the following chart.

Required Actions	Target Date	Assessment Method and Criteria	Evaluator(s)

D. *Explanation of consequences*: Be clear about what will happen if your student teacher fails to fulfill requirements. Follow university procedures. Allow student teacher ample time to ask questions, express concerns, and give input.

E. *Closing*: Close the conference with words of hope and encouragement.

Sample Conference

Date: ___2/1/03___ Time: 4 to 5 p.m. Location: Room 112 Hanson High School
People Present: Student teacher and her program advisor, cooperating teacher,
university supervisor

A. *Opening*:

1. *Introductions if necessary*:
   "Thank you all for coming. Janice, we're glad you've brought your advisor. Let's make introductions before we begin."

2. *Purpose of the conference*:
   "As you know, we have been struggling with some problems during your student teaching experience. We're meeting here today to clarify expectations, discuss ways for you to meet them, and explain what will happen if the concerns aren't addressed."

3. *Context statement:*
   "We know that you have been working hard, and it hasn't been easy. We have seen growth in your one-on-one relationships with students. We're concerned, though, about some other important issues."

B. *Communication of concern*:

1. *Overview of concerns*:
   "Two things are causing me the most concern. First, I am worried about your lack of preparation and tardiness. You are also struggling with planning and delivery of lessons."

2. *Specific concerns:*

Explain Concern	Check for Understanding	Student Teacher's Questions and Concerns
"You were late to school six times in the past two weeks. It is also a problem when you are late or come in right when the period begins with the students. Yesterday you were early only for fifth period. This is a reflection of professionalism."	"Does this match your perception? Do you understand how this relates to professionalism?"	"What questions or concerns do you have about this?"
"Your planning isn't thorough enough and, because you don't have your lessons prepared on time, I can't give feedback in advance."	"What value do you see in my looking over your plans? What are other ways I could help you?"	What questions or concerns do you have about this?

C. *Plan for improvement*: Discuss ways to address and assess concerns. The team— including student teacher—completes chart.

Required Actions	Target Date	Assessment Method and Criteria	Evaluator(s)
Eliminate tardiness.	Review in 2 weeks	Recorded observations. Must be on time every day to every class.	Cooperating teacher
The day before teaching a lesson, submit the lesson plan in the morning.	Review in 2 weeks	Lesson plan reviewed daily. It must be clear, detailed, and focused on appropriate objectives.	Cooperating teacher and university supervisor (weekly)
Discuss plans with cooperating teacher and incorporate suggestions or requests.	Review in 2 weeks	Lesson observation. Suggestions must be evident in enacted plans. Evidence of reduced student misbehavior (increase in time on task) and achievement of student learning objectives (complete lesson assessments).	Cooperating teacher (daily) and university supervisor (weekly)

D. *Explanation of consequences*:
   "If you meet these requirements, you will be able to continue in the program. If you are unable to meet them, we will discuss your options, which may include your decision to withdraw from the program or our decision to remove you. We want to make sure that you understand that this is serious. You have to meet standards for licensure."

E. *Closing*:
   "We've seen progress in other areas and we think you can do it here, too. What would be helpful to you? We will do all we can to help you meet these goals."

10

Growing as a Professional

"The good mentor is a model of a continuous learner. . . . Good mentor teachers are transparent about their own search for better answers and more effective solutions to their own problems. They model this commitment by their openness to learn from colleagues, including beginning teachers, and by their willingness to pursue professional growth through a variety of means. Most important, they share new knowledge and perplexing questions with their beginning teachers in a collegial manner."

—Rowley, 1999, p. 22

Congratulations to you for completing the reading of this text, and perhaps now or perhaps a bit later, for successfully mentoring a new professional. At the end of your mentoring partnership, you will most likely feel pleased about and maybe even a bit proud of the changes you see in your new teacher partner's professional development. And, by serving as a mentor, you may have developed professionally as well (Huling & Resta, 2001). Well-trained mentors are a tremendously important facet of both preservice and induction teacher education. You have knowledge, skills, and attitudes that can be put to use in numerous settings and that can serve as the launching pad for myriad other professional development opportunities for you. This chapter explores just a few ways to further your professional development. This chapter addresses action research, collaborations, and advanced certification and degrees.

> "It's what you learn after you know it all that counts."
>
> —John Wooden
> (quoted in Creative Quotations, 2002)

> **Note to the reader:**
> **Before you continue** . . .
>
> We know that many readers have experience with some of the professional development opportunities we describe in this chapter. Skip the "been there, done that" sections and use your time instead to talk with your new teacher partner about his or her plans for continuing professional development. Or, read those sections anyway and see if we have it right.

ACTION RESEARCH

Teachers can ask and answer questions related to their practice through a powerful inquiry process called action, or participatory, research.

Defining Action Research

Action research is conducted by teachers seeking to learn about and improve their own teaching activities (Gay & Airasian, 2000) or those wanting to learn about classroom life from their students' perspective. As is true of other forms of research, action research is a process of organized, reflective inquiry that pursues issues of interest through the collection and analysis of tangible data. Action research's focus is upon improving practice in immediate ways or upon improving the quality of people's lives in their organizations by encouraging participation in shared inquiry (Cresswell, 2002). The textbox gives some titles of recent studies that illustrate the data-driven, participant-focused, action-oriented nature of such studies.

Action research has tremendous potential to improve schooling and professional development for a number of reasons:

> **Sample Action Research Projects: Titles From**
>
> *Networks: An Online Journal for Teacher Research*
>
> (Volumes 4 and 5; 2001, 2002)
> (Journal available at www.oise.utoronto.ca/~ctd/networks/journal/)
>
> - Using Concept Maps to Aid Reading Comprehension in a High School Biology Classroom
> - Infusing Computer Technology: A Novice Teacher User Meets the Challenge with High School ESL Students
> - The Story of Their Lives: Understanding Our Students' Literacy Practices and Events

- Action research allows teachers to call into question norms, practices, and policies that may otherwise be enacted without examination.
- Whereas some formal research may seem distant and lacking in generalizability for classroom teachers, action research is grounded in the teacher's local context of concern, with all its quirks and complexities.
- Action research can provide a voice for students, too, as they become involved in studying and shaping the classroom world around them through shared research projects.
- Action research projects can encourage collaboration through faculty teams, thus enhancing collegiality and shared professional discourse.
- Action research can enhance teachers' sense of efficacy: the firmly held conviction that they have the power and ability to make a difference, to better their world by improving learning and classroom life for their students.

Conducting Action Research

Action research is similar to formal educational research in that it must be systematic (planned and organized using a logical approach), it begins with a question, and it involves the collection and scrutiny of data. Teacher reflection plays a critical role in action research; teachers reflect on data and thus reexamine their research questions, methods, and the resultant changes they may enact. The steps of research are often nonlinear because critical reflection at any point can modify the future direction of the study. In addition, one study's results can lead to the next study's questions. Nonetheless, the general approach is to formulate a problem, devise a plan that addresses that problem, institute an intervention (or new approach), and assess the effects of the intervention.

Gay and Airasian (2000) give helpful advice for the four stages of action research.

1. *Ask a question based on some aspect of your practice.* Questions should be narrowly focused so that it is feasible for them to be addressed with the time and resources at your disposal. Sample questions include:

- "During my lessons do I give equal verbal attention to my male and female students?"
- "What kind of homework assignments do my students and their families value?"
- "Would using graphic organizers improve my students' comprehension of the material in the social studies text?"
- "Might using a classroom meeting model decrease the incidence of arguments in my room?"
- "How might we as a school better recognize the expertise of the families we serve?"

Note that each of these questions seems to be based on some underlying problem perceived by the teacher or by other members of the school community. The area of focus should be one about which you feel passionate and over which you have some control (Mills, 2000). The more focused and specific the question, the more amenable it is to empirical study through action research.

2. *Develop and carry out a plan to gather evidence related to the question.* Select methods of collecting data that are appropriate for your question and that will reap actual evidence that can be analyzed after the heat of the classroom moment. Examples of data-collection strategies are recordings (e.g., photographs taken and audio and video recordings made in the classroom), student or family questionnaires and other reports of their experiences (collected anonymously when the study calls for it), student performance data (e.g., test scores or essay reports), and observation data gathered by another person (e.g., classroom traffic pattern mappings, tally marks of student comments, or scripting of your verbal behaviors). Each of these data-collection strategies should be highly focused and structured. Interpretation will be easier and more closely related to your question as a result. Also, triangulating data (that is, comparing several sources of related information) can help protect the validity of your study.

In developing the data collection plan, consider building in the ability to compare data. For example, in the graphic organizers question, above, you could collect "baseline" data on student performance before using graphic organizers (such as diagrams and charts) to compare with data you gather after your intervention of using graphic organizers. In the question on equal participation, it would be helpful for you to write predictions of what you think you will find through research. Comparison of data can help to minimize bias in your study.

3. *Make decisions based on the data you collect.* Interpreting your data begins with activities such a tallying student responses, comparing scores before and after the intervention, or coding and finding themes in written responses or oral histories. It can be helpful to share preliminary analyses with the participants or your colleagues to ensure that you have considered alternative inferences based on the data. Your analysis will yield a tentative answer to your research question and information that can allow you to make decisions based on this aspect of practice. As you make decisions based on your findings, remember to keep the potential changes in scale with the scope of the study and with an eye toward its limitations.

4. *Take action.* Use what you have discovered to change your practice and perhaps to ask a question that will fuel the next action research project. By engaging in a new phase of research, you illustrate the cyclic nature of action research that alternates between action and reflection, with later cycles refining the data collection and interpretation as a result of reflection on earlier attempts (Dick, 1999).

Getting Going in Action Research: A Few Tips

Some induction programs require new teachers and their experienced teacher partners to engage in action research. For others, conducting research will be a new endeavor. If this is your first foray into the field, a few tips may help you get going in action research:

1. *Build a team.* Talking informally with colleagues is a good way to clarify your thinking and to gain new perspectives on an issue. More formally, developing a team of researchers who conduct a shared project or pursue individual ones can provide a professional community. Even selecting a single partner can enrich the research experience. Imagine how the dynamics of your relationship with your new teacher partner might change if you were to embark on a classroom study together.

2. *Choose your question by carefully reflecting on life at school.* Action research projects typically are designed to address a perceived discrepancy between the way life *should be* and the way *it is*. If you are considering action research, try taking notes for a week or so, jotting down the time of day, circumstance, and topic of your puzzlement, sense of disquiet, or frustration. Analyze your notes to find the themes in your concerns and to formulate in the clearest language possible the thing you want to know. You might, for instance, narrow your issue down to the fact that your students seem inattentive and restless during your social studies lessons. Select the question that would allow you to improve some corner of the world and address your need to know. For example, your social studies issue may give rise to the question: "What instructional strategies are preferred by my eighth-grade social studies students?"

3. *Check your study for limited perspective taking.* What may be a big problem for you may be experienced by your students or their families as completely nonproblematic. Think about your study from different perspectives to ensure that you are working to change something that is valued by others or at least that it does not make faulty assumptions about others. For instance, a primary-grade teacher may have captured her issue with a sense of exasperation: "My students are just not internally motivated! What can I do to help them want to learn?" Examining the issue from the students' perspective may result in a different question entirely: "Our

teacher asks us to do so many things that we do not care about at all. What can we do about that?" Reading professional literature or involving others openly and actively in your study can help you think about possible limitations in your perspective or assumptions.

COLLABORATION

Collaborations can be fleeting and informal or lasting and highly structured, but commitment to a set of shared goals is increasingly a necessity in the profession of education. To help students learn and to sustain a high quality of life for the participants of schooling, teachers must collaborate with each other and with other agencies, individuals, and institutions. This section explores just a few forms of collaboration that may enhance your professional development.

> "The way a team plays as a whole determines its success. You may have the greatest bunch of individual stars in the world, but if they don't play together, the club won't be worth a dime."
>
> —Babe Ruth
> (quoted in Creative Quotations, 2002)

Peer Collaborations

Peer collaborations can take many forms. Informal mentor–mentor conversations, team teaching situations, reading groups, and lesson study are examples.

By its nature, your work as a mentor or cooperating teacher places you in a collaborative situation where you study and discuss teaching with an inexperienced peer. Do you and your mentor peers have the opportunity to share your experiences and to discuss important issues related to mentoring? Cooperating teachers who participated in a recent academy told us clearly that one of the most appreciated outcomes of the academy was the structured time to network with cooperating teacher peers from other schools and districts. Rarely do these cooperating teachers have the opportunity to talk freely about issues of shared concern related to their roles as mentors.

Though it is indeed difficult to structure time for these conversations, we have seen a few successful strategies that can be implemented without a great deal of preparation or cost. In one credential program, for instance, the cooperating teachers at a school site meet every other Monday for a brown bag lunch to discuss issues related to mentoring. The university supervisor facilitates the conversation, and the site's student teachers cover the classrooms for the 20-minute period of overlap during the cooperating teachers' staggered lunch schedule. In another, cooperating teachers from a number of sites spend a couple hours together to celebrate the end of the semester and to enjoy each other's company in a social setting.

The university or induction program is probably vitally interested in your having occasion to interact with other mentors and can often facilitate these opportunities. A request from you to the university supervisor or program coordinator may launch the process. If the university is unable to assist, see what you can do as a group of mentors to carve out opportunities to meet, however infrequently. Meetings such as these are critical for increasing shared problem solving and enhancing the knowledge base of mentoring.

You may also elect to participate in collaborations aimed toward enhancing your classroom performance or overall professionalism. Some sites have teacher reading groups where members discuss a brief professional article about once a month. One member each month is responsible for selecting and duplicating the article and leading the discussion. Articles selected should explore controversial or current topics, and sharing can be structured (where everyone gives the same format of feedback, e.g., "One thing I learned . . ." ; "One thing I wondered. . .") or informal. Sometimes the groups even read the assignments *during* the meetings. Keeping the reading assignments short and manageable allows the group to continue to flourish.

> "Individual commitment to a group effort—that is what makes a team work, a company work, a society work, a civilization work."
>
> —Vince Lombardi
> (quoted in Creative Quotations, 2002)

In an approach that centers more directly on classroom practice, teachers in other countries (namely, Japan) and in America are examining their practice through lesson study. In lesson study, a teacher spends an extensive time carefully planning a "research lesson" in any subject area, usually in collaboration with study team members. Then he or she teaches it to students while group members observe. The lesson, which becomes the focal point of research into the teacher's practice, is thoroughly prepared because it will be closely observed. The lesson's events are typically recorded through several means, such as members' observational notes and audio recordings. After the lesson, the group discusses it in a colloquium.

Although lesson study seems simple, it can be responsible for a wide variety of educational and professional outcomes. Lewis (2000) observed that lesson study allowed teachers in Japan to develop individually, to increase in their ability to observe children and their learning, to spread new content and approaches to other teachers, and to connect individual teacher's practices to school goals and broader goals as well. Though it begins with intense attention given to a single lesson, the effort spreads to improvement for other teachers and can shape policies in the school and society as well. Its focus recognizes the centrality of teachers and their work in improving learning for students, and it provides a powerful example of what teachers can do through collaboration.

Professional Community Collaborations: Teacher Education Accreditation

The National Council for the Accreditation of Teacher Education (NCATE) offers voluntary accreditation to colleges and universities that educate teachers at the undergraduate, postbaccalaureate, or graduate levels. NCATE's accreditation process is predicated on a set of unit standards that define quality preparation for teachers. One standard requires collaboration between the university and its partners (that is you) in the design, implementation, and evaluation of field-based experiences (NCATE, 2002). At the "target" level of performance, collaboration between institutions that educate teachers (the university and the school site) is so strong that resources, expertise, and professional development activities are integrated across the institutions to support the development of teachers.

Teacher education institutions that do not pursue NCATE accreditation are nonetheless required to meet state accreditation standards, and those standards frequently include collaboration among participants in the design, implementation, and evaluation of field-based portions of the teacher education program. Another venue for experienced teachers to collaborate for the improvement of education, then, is involvement in the processes by which institutions of higher education prepare teachers.

ADVANCED CERTIFICATION AND DEGREES

Advanced study can result in a larger and more specialized body of professional knowledge and skills, enhanced practice, greater job authority, and better personal and professional satisfaction. It can also result in a greater number of options available to teachers as they make choices about how to contribute to their profession. Formally, further study can lead to certification (including additional licensure) or to advanced degrees.

Certification

Teachers can pursue a number of certificates that support their instructional practices or that enrich their professional well-being in other ways. Examples of the many certificates available include certificates for computer-enhanced instruction, gifted and talented education, instruction for learners who are acquiring English, reading instruction, and Web-based instructional design. Independent and public colleges and private organizations offer these certificates through options ranging from traditional face-to-face instruction to totally online delivery. To find certificate programs of interest to you, you can speak with your colleagues or university partners, or you can check print and online information. Meta search engines can make Internet exploration easy; you might try one of the four engines listed in Exercise 1.3. Search terms or phrases such as "certificate programs for teachers" or "ESL certificate" can start your exploration.

Another form of voluntary certification for teachers is gaining in momentum across America: National Board certification. Administered by the National Board for Professional Teaching Standards (NBPTS), National Board certification complements state licensure of beginning teachers with advanced, standards-based certification for experienced teachers. Teachers elect certification at various developmental levels (e.g., Early Childhood or Adolescence and Young Adulthood) and in particular fields or subjects (e.g., art, mathematics, generalist, or exceptional needs).

Each of the sets of standards that drive National Board certificates is based on five core propositions of teaching, put forth by the Board in its 1989 policy statement: What Teachers Should Know and Be Able to Do (see textbox for the propositions). Though these propositions are expressed in succinct language in just five sentences, they codify an impressive knowledge base, set of skills, and preferred dispositions for skilled teachers. For example, the first proposition holds that teachers advocate

**Five Core Propositions
(NBPTS, 2002)**

The five core propositions of teaching, which have remained the same since they were put forth in 1989, are the following:

1. Teachers are committed to students and their learning.

2. Teachers know the subjects they teach and how to teach those subjects to students.

3. Teachers are responsible for managing and monitoring student learning.

4. Teachers think systematically about their practice and learn from experience.

5. Teachers are members of learning communities.

for their students, hold high expectations for them all, treat them fairly, and use information about them as people and learners to adjust instruction. Commitment to learners also requires that teachers understand learning and development and encourage students to grow holistically and as individuals who respect each other and their responsibilities to society. The other propositions hold similarly high expectations for teachers.

The process of National Board certification spans many months and includes two major components. First, candidates prepare a professional portfolio that includes video footage of their teaching and analyzes aspects of their classroom work. Second, candidates take a written examination that explores their professional knowledge, skills and judgment. Many universities offer graduate study related to the National Boards, and other educational agencies, such as county offices of education, offer support to candidates. Financial support and public recognition for teachers preparing for certification varies across the nation by state and by local policy. Incentives can include fee support, salary supplements, and license portability. The demanding and lengthy process entailed in National Board certification is meant to provide educators with an opportunity similar to one found by professionals in other fields: the opportunity to achieve distinction through a rigorous external review of their professional work.

Finally, advanced certification can result in additional licenses or credentials. For instance, educational specialists in special education or in educational leadership require advanced credentials. Such study often overlaps with graduate degrees.

Graduate Degrees

Graduate study at the master's or doctoral level provides another way to deepen your professional understandings and contribute to your profession. If you are weighing the question of *whether* to pursue graduate study, think about your possible objections. If they include the concern that a program could mean too many years of hard work, we remind you that in a few years, you will be a few years older. You can be older *with* the degree, or older *without* it.

Selecting a degree. A master's degree signifies that one has *mastered* the habits of inquiry and advanced knowledge in one's field, and the doctoral degree indicates that, in addition to completing extensive study, one has conducted original research or other work in the field. Master's degree programs are shorter in length than doctoral programs and often serve as prerequisites for doctoral programs. Doctoral degrees include the Doctor of Philosophy (Ph.D.), which typically serves as preparation for a career in research or scholarship, and the Educational Doctorate (Ed.D.), which often prepares scholarly practitioners for leadership in education.

Which advanced degree is right for you? We often ask teachers what they hope to be doing in ten years. If they see themselves continuing their work in the classroom, then the master's degree is often appropriate, though some people holding doctoral degrees do in fact continue their work in the classroom. For instance, if a teacher finds tremendous satisfaction in coaching new teachers, he or she may pursue a master's degree with an emphasis in staff development. With this degree, a teacher can continue teaching in the classroom but have the added knowledge and skills to accompany his or her work as a mentor. If, instead, teachers hope to work at the district level, or if they would like to work with teachers through a university position, then the doctorate is probably the appropriate choice. Factors such as family situation (e.g., the age of the teacher's children) also factor into this important decision.

Selecting an institution. As is the case in selecting a degree to pursue, many factors may weigh into choosing an institution. A few of these considerations are listed in the textbox. As you ponder these questions, we would like to offer a few pieces of advice. First, as you select your area of study, we suggest that you pick one that fuels a professional passion for you. Graduate study involves a large personal investment and in a sense commits (or at least enables) you to contribute to your field in new ways. Your selection of an area of study should reflect that serious commitment and interest.

> **Choosing an Institution for an Advanced Degree: A Few Questions to Ask**
>
> √ In what area would I like to specialize?
> √ What is the quality of the institution?
> √ Does the institution's mission match my own?
> √ Does the institution's physical proximity and course schedule match my needs?
> √ What kind of support does the institution provide for its students?

Second, as you select an institution, we urge you to choose one that will open opportunities for you rather than closing them. Choosing a maximally convenient program from a questionable institution may save you time now, but it may close doors to you in the future if the degree is not recognized or well regarded by the professional community. Institutions of higher education are increasingly offering "fast track" advanced degree programs that take less time than traditional programs or that never require you to set foot in a classroom. Plenty of reputable institutions offer solid graduate degrees through student-convenient delivery systems. However, many less reputable institutions do so as well. Thoroughly investigate programs before you commit. Is the institution accredited? By whom? As discussed previously, universities can elect to undergo national accreditation through the National Council for the Accreditation of Teacher Education; minimally, they should have regional accreditation by a recognized accrediting body. Investigate the mission and reputation of institutions as well. You can read ratings of programs, and you can talk with colleagues to assess institutions' strengths and drawbacks. Many Web sites are devoted to helping potential graduate students select institutions that meet their goals and personal priorities; see Box 10.1 for three such sites. Two are commercial sites, so expect advertisements and always read critically.

Box 10.1   Searching the Internet to Investigate Degree Programs

---

www.gradschools.com

This site provides comprehensive information related to graduate schools. Allows you to search by geographical region, type of program (academic area), certificate programs, and online programs.

www.petersons.com

Peterson's is an online educational resource that touts itself as comprehensive. The "Grad Channel" (select "Graduate Programs" from the home page) allows you to search by subject and school. It includes online programs.

www.utexas.edu/world/univ/

Web U.S. Higher Education is sponsored by the University of Texas at Austin. It lists universities and community colleges by state and alphabetically.

PARTING WORDS

"The beginning is always today."

—Mary Shelley Wollstonecraft
(quoted in Creative Quotations, 2002)

We opened Chapter 1 by thanking you for picking up this book and turning to the first chapter. We close the book by thanking you for reading through to its last chapter. Thank you for doing work that is critical to the profession of education by mentoring a student teacher or newly credentialed teacher. Thank you for embarking on this journey of professional development, and thank you for allowing us to accompany you. Good wishes to you as you continue to grow, to develop, and to sustain new professionals through your caring support.

EXERCISES

Exercise 10.1   Personal Professional Inquiries

This chapter suggested many collaborative and formal approaches for inquiring into the art and science of teaching. We know that teachers also inquire into teaching individually and that such informal individual inquiries can also add to the knowledge base and inform teaching. Go through this checklist to reflect on the ways you are learning about teaching. For each inquiry, mark in the table's middle column a checkmark (if it's a strategy you use), an asterisk (if it's a strategy you plan on trying), or a slash (if it's a strategy that does not work for you). Add your own strategies to the list. Share your ideas with your new teacher partner to instill the expectation that good teachers are constant learners.

Marks:

√ = *a strategy I use*

* = *a strategy I plan on trying*

/ = *a strategy that does not work for me*

Inquiry	Mark	Recent Example or Note to Self
Read professional journals.		
Read information on the Internet.		
Write (e.g., journal entries, poetry, articles).		
Videotape my teaching and analyze the tape.		
Approach a peer or other professional for a new perspective.		
Observe a peer.		
Attend a workshop.		
Attend a conference.		
Take a class.		
Conduct action research.		
Engage in lesson study.		

Exercise 10.2   Inquiring Into Action Research

Find out more about action research. Here are a few options:

1. Browse the Internet to read some sample research studies. Try search terms such as "action research journals." (One source—*Networks: An Online Journal for Teacher Research,* Volumes 4 and 5; 2001, 2002—is found in the "Sample Action Research Projects" sidebar earlier in this chapter.)

2. Contact a person with expertise, either at your site or at the university. Ask who teaches the research methods courses. Share your initial question about what you would like to study, and ask for advice regarding feasibility, data collection, and data analysis.

3. Ask a colleague on site or your new teacher partner to try a small-scale study with you.

4. Talk with your students about a project you might pursue as a class. Research into the local community is a great way to address important social studies content and skills (e.g., taking oral histories) and can build tighter connections between school, home, and neighborhood as well.

5. Conduct your own study and submit it to a journal for action research (perhaps a source that you ran across in option 1 of this list.)

Exercise 10.3   Investigating National Board Certification

If you or your partner is interested in National Board certification, take your pick from three options:

1. If you are a Board-certified teacher, walk your new teacher partner through the process, sharing your motivations for pursuing certification, the procedures, and the important consequences you have experienced (positive and negative, if any).

2. If National Board certification is new for you, spend some time investigating the Web site of the National Board for Professional Teaching Standards: www.nbpts.org. Which certificate would you pursue? Choosing "Standards & National Board Certification" on the main page and clicking on the "State & Local Support & Incentives" link on the subsequent page leads you to information about incentives your state and district may offer for certification.

3. Interview a teacher who has achieved or attempted National Board certification. Why did he or she pursue the process? What does the certification signify? What did the teacher learn from the process? How, if at all, has it enhanced his or her professional experience?

Exercise 10.4 Building and Sharing Professional Portfolios

Many teacher education programs, an increasing number of school districts, and National Board certification require teacher candidates to construct professional portfolios. Portfolios are collections of evidence and reflections on that evidence that convey in rich and varied ways teachers' commitments and capabilities. Building a professional portfolio can support growth for teachers at all points in the career continuum.

Constructing the Portfolio

1. Collect evidence that reveals who you are and what you can do as a teacher.

2. Organize the artifacts according to some scheme.

3. Write a brief reflection of what each artifact reveals about you as a professional.

Sharing the Portfolio

1. Exchange portfolios with another portfolio author, such as your new teacher partner or an experienced colleague, and allow time for review.

2. Begin your portfolio conversation with appreciative commentary on what the author knows or can do in the domains represented. Focus less on evaluation or missing information than on description of the evidence present.

3. Draw the conversation to a close by discussing what the author learned by composing and reflecting on his or her portfolio. Also talk about future goals suggested by the portfolio.

Sample Professional Portfolio Artifacts	
<ul><li>A brief opening: a philosophy or credo of teaching</li><li>Teacher examination scores</li><li>Lesson plans and evaluations</li><li>Unit plans</li><li>Principal or peer observations</li><li>Sample student work</li><li>Pictures depicting the classroom environment</li><li>Evidence of professional involvement</li><li>Your work in exercises from earlier chapters of this book</li></ul>	<ul><li>Sample student assessments</li><li>Professional subscriptions</li><li>Academic transcripts</li><li>Professional credentials</li><li>Letters to parents</li><li>Photographs of students at work</li><li>Evidence of instruction that meets the needs of individual students</li><li>Awards</li></ul> (These are randomly ordered. How would you organize them?)

Exercise 10.5 Revising the Book

You know much about teaching and about the knowledge, skills, and dispositions necessary for a mentor. How would you revise this book? What was helpful? What was missing? We would enjoy hearing from you!

References

Acheson, K. A., & Gall, M. A. (1992). *Techniques in the clinical supervision of teachers* (3rd ed.). New York: Longman.

American Evaluation Association. (1994). *Guiding principles for evaluators.* Retrieved June 10, 2002, from www.eval.org/EvaluationDocuments/aeaprin6.html

Barrett, J. (1986). Evaluation of student teachers. *ERIC Digest 13* [online]. Retrieved June 15, 2002, from www.ed.gov/databases/ERIC_Digests/ed278658.html

Berliner, D. C. (1988). Implications of studies of expertise in pedagogy for teacher education and evaluation. In *New directions for teacher assessment* (Proceedings of the 1988 ETS Invitational Conference, pp. 39–68). Princeton, NJ: Educational Testing Service.

Berquist, W. H., & Phillips, S. R. (1975). *A handbook for faculty development: Vol. I.* Dansville, NY: The Council for the Advancement of Small College.

Borko, H., & Mayfield, V. (1995). The roles of the cooperating teacher and university supervisor in learning to teach. *Teaching and Teacher Education, 11*(5), 501–518.

Brinko, K. T. (1990, April). *Optimal conditions for effective feedback.* Paper presented at the annual meeting of the American Educational Research Association, Boston, MA.

Brookfield, S. (1986). *Understanding and facilitating adult learning.* San Francisco: Jossey-Bass.

Bullough, R. V., Jr., Hobbs, S. F., Kauchak, D. P., Crow, N. A., & Stokes, D. (1997). Long-term PDS development in research universities and the clinicalization of teacher education. *Journal of Teacher Education, 48*(2) 85–95.

Burden, P. R. (1990). Teacher development. In W. R. Houston (Ed.), *Handbook of research on teacher education* (pp. 311–328). New York: Macmillan.

Buzzelli, C., & Johnston, B. (2001). Authority, power, and morality in classroom discourse. *Teaching and Teacher Education, 17,* 873–884.

Calderhead, J. (1991). The nature and growth of knowledge in student teaching. *Teaching and Teacher Education, 7,* 531–535.

California Department of Education. (2002). Continuum of support provider guidance. *Beginning Teacher Support and Assessment Principles and Orientation Training Manual.*

California State University, Fullerton. (2002). *California State University teacher evaluation form.* Fullerton: Author.

Carr, J. F., & Harris, D. E. (2001). *Succeeding with standards: Linking curriculum, assessment, and action planning.* Alexandria, VA: Association for Supervision and Curriculum Development.

Charles, C. (1996). *Building classroom discipline* (5th ed.). White Plains, NY: Longman.

Chubbuck, S. M., Clift, R. T., Allard, J., & Quinlan, J. (2001). Playing it safe as a novice teacher: Implications for programs for new teachers. *Journal of Teacher Education, 52*(5), 365–376.

Connor, K., & Killmer, N. (1995, October). *Evaluation of cooperating teacher effectiveness.* Paper presented at the annual meeting of the Midwest Educational Research Association, Chicago, IL.

Creative Quotations [searchable quotations database]. (2002). Retrieved October 7, 2002, from www.creativequotations.com

Cresswell, J. W. (2002). *Educational research: Planning, conducting, and evaluating quantitative and qualitative research.* Upper Saddle River, NJ: Merrill Prentice Hall.

Cruickshank, D. R., Bainer, D. K., & Metcalf, K. K. (1999). *The act of teaching* (2nd ed.). Boston: McGraw-Hill College.

Cushing, K. S., Sabers, D. S., & Berliner, D. C. (1992). Olympic gold: Investigations of expertise in teaching. *Educational Horizons, 70*(3), 108–114.

Daane, C. J. (2000). Clinical Master Teacher program: Teachers' and interns' perceptions of supervision with limited university intervention. *Action in Teacher Education, 22*(1), 93–100.

Danielson, C. (1996). *Enhancing professional practice: A framework for teaching.* Alexandria, VA: Association for Supervision and Curriculum Development.

Danielson, C., & McGreal, T. L. (2000). *Teacher evaluation to enhance professional practice.* Alexandria, VA: Association for Supervision and Curriculum Development.

Darling-Hammond, L. (1996). The quiet revolution: Rethinking teacher development. *Educational Leadership, 53*(6), 4–10.

Davidman, L., & Davidman, P. T. (1997). *Teaching with a multicultural perspective: A practical guide.* New York: Longman.

Dick, B. (1999). *What is action research?* Retrieved June 10, 2002, from www.scu.edu.au/schools/gcm/ar/whatisar.html

Doyle, W. (1986). Classroom organization and management. In M. Wittrock (Ed.), *Handbook of research on teaching* (3rd ed., pp. 393–431). New York: Macmillan.

Duffy, D. G. (1998, June). Teaching and the balancing of round stones. *Phi Delta Kappan, 79,* 777–780.

Eisner, E. (1982). An artistic approach to supervision. In T. J. Sergiovanni (Ed.), *Supervision of teaching* (pp. 53–66). Alexandria, VA: Association for Supervision and Curriculum Development.

Fenstermacher, G. D. (1990). Some moral considerations on teaching as a profession. In J. I. Goodlad, R. Soder, & K. A. Sirotnik (Eds.), *The moral dimensions of teaching.* San Francisco: Jossey-Bass.

Fuller, F. F. (1969). Concerns of teachers: A developmental conceptualization. *American Educational Research Journal, 6,* 207–226.

Fuller, F. F., & Bown, O. H. (1975). Becoming a teacher. In K. Ryan (Ed.), *Teacher education (74th yearbook of the National Society for the Study of Education,* Pt. II, pp. 25–53). Chicago: University of Chicago.

Fulwiler, L. (1996). A beggar in both worlds: A supervisor in the schools and the university. *Journal of Teacher Education, 47*(1), 21–26.

Garman, N. B. (1982). The clinical approach to supervision. In T. J. Sergiovanni (Ed.), *Supervision of teaching* (pp. 35–52). Alexandria, VA: Association for Supervision and Curriculum Development.

Gay, L. R. (1992). *Educational Research: Competencies for Analysis and Application* (4th ed.). New York: Merrill.

Gay, L. R., & Airasian, P. (2000). *Educational research: Competencies for analysis and application* (6th ed.). Upper Saddle River, NJ: Merrill Prentice Hall.

Gonzalez, N., Andrade, R., Civil, M., & Moll, L. (2001). Bridging funds of distributed knowledge: Creating zones of practices in mathematics. *Journal of Education for Students Placed at Risk (JESPAR), 6*(1–2), 115–132.

Good, T. L., & Brophy, J. E. (1994). *Looking in classrooms* (6th ed.). New York: HarperCollins College Publishers.

Goodlad, J. I. (1990). The occupation of teaching in schools. In J. I. Goodlad, R. Soder, & K A. Sirotnik (Eds.), *The moral dimensions of teaching.* San Francisco: Jossey-Bass.

Gotliffe, A. (1994). What your student teacher wants you to know. *Instructor, 104*(1), 82–83.

Greene, M. (1973). *Teacher as stranger: Educational philosophy for the modern age.* Belmont, CA: Wadsworth.

Guillaume, A. M., & Rudney, G. L. (1993). Student teachers' growth toward independence: An analysis of their changing concerns. *Journal of Teaching and Teacher Education, 9*, 65–80.

Guillaume, A. M., & Rudney, G. L. (2002, April). *Faith, feedback and freedom: Student teachers' preferences for cooperating teachers' characteristics and behaviors.* Paper presented at the annual meeting of the American Educational Research Association, New Orleans, LA.

Herman, J. L., Aschbacher, P. R., & Winters, L. (1992) *A practical guide to alternative assessment.* Alexandria, VA: Association for Supervision and Curriculum Development.

Howe, K. R. (1986). A conceptual basis for ethics in teacher education. *Journal of Teacher Education, 37*(3), 5–12.

Huling, L., & Resta, V. (2001). *Teacher mentoring as professional development.* Washington, D.C.: ERIC Clearinghouse on Teaching and Teacher Education. (ERIC Document Reproduction Service No. EDO-SP-2001–4)

Interstate New Teacher Assessment and Support Consortium. (1992). Retrieved June 10, 2002, from www.ccsso.org/intascst.html

Jackson, P. W. (1968). *Life in classrooms.* New York: Holt, Rinehart & Winston.

Jackson, P. W. (1986). *The practice of teaching.* New York: Teachers College Press.

Kagan, D. M. (1992). Professional growth among preservice and beginning teachers. *Review of Educational Research, 62*(2), 129–169.

Kagan, S. (1994). *Cooperative learning.* San Juan Capistrano, CA: Kagan Cooperative Learning.

Kauffman, D. (1992). Supervision of student teachers. *ERIC Digest* [online]. Retrieved June 15, 2002, from www.ed.gov/databases/ERIC_Digests/ed344873.html

Kidder, R. M., & Born, P. L. (1998–1999, December–January). Resolving ethical dilemmas in the classroom. *Educational Leadership, 56*(4), 38–41.

Knowles, M. S. (1980). *The modern practice of adult education: From pedagogy to andragogy* (2nd ed.). Chicago: Association/Follett.

Knowles, M. S. (1984). *Andragogy in action: Applying modern principles of adult learning.* San Francisco: Jossey-Bass.

Koerner, M. E. (1992). The cooperating teacher: An ambivalent participant in student teaching. *Journal of Teacher Education, 43*, 46–56.

Lampert, M. (1985). How do teachers manage to teach? Perspectives on problems in practice. *Harvard Educational Review, 55*(2), 178–194.

Lasley, T. (1996). Mentors: They simply believe. *Peabody Journal of Education, 71*(1), 64–70.

Lewis, C. (2000, April). *Lesson Study: The Core of Japanese Professional Development.* Invited address at the annual meeting of the American Educational Research Association, New Orleans, LA.

McNeil, J. D. (1982). A scientific approach to supervision. In T. J. Sergiovanni (Ed.), *Supervision of teaching* (pp. 18–34). Alexandria, VA: Association for Supervision and Curriculum Development.

Mills, G. E. (2000). *Action research: A guide for the teacher researcher.* Upper Saddle River, NJ: Merrill Prentice Hall.

Moll, L. C., Amanti, C., Neff, D., & Gonzalez, N. (1992). Funds of knowledge for teaching: Using a qualitative approach to connect homes and classrooms. *Theory into Practice, 31*, 132-141.

National Board for Professional Teaching Standards. (2002). Retrieved June 13, 2002, from www.nbpts.org/about/coreprops.cfm

National Council for the Accreditation of Teacher Education. (2001). *Professional standards for the accreditation of schools, colleges, and departments of education.* Washington, D.C.: Author.

National Council for the Accreditation of Teacher Education. (2002). Retrieved June 13, 2002, from www.ncate.org/standard/m_stds.htm

Networks: An online journal for teacher research (Vols. 4 and 5; 2001, 2002). Retrieved June 10, 2002, from www.oise.utoronto.ca/~ctd/networks/journal/

Nieto, S. (1996). *Affirming diversity: The sociopolitical context of multicultural education* (2nd ed.). White Plains, NY: Longman.

Ogle, D. (1986). K-W-L: A teaching model that develops active reading of expository text. *The Reading Teacher, 39*, 564–570.

An Online Library of Literature. (2002). Retrieved October 28, 2002, from www.literature.org/authors/tolstoy-leo/anna-karenina/part-01/chapter-01.html

Page, M. L., Rudney, G. L., & Marxen, C. E. (2002, April). *Preparing successful beginning teachers: Advocacy, gatekeeping, and teachability.* Paper presented at the annual meeting of the American Educational Research Association, New Orleans, LA.

Pigge, F. L., & Marso, R. N. (1987). Relationships between student characteristics and changes in attitudes, concerns, anxieties, and confidence about teaching during teacher preparation. *Journal of Educational Research, 81*, 109–115.

Rice, E. H. (2002). The collaboration process in professional development schools: Results of a meta-ethnography, 1990–1998. *Journal of Teacher Education, 53*(1), 55–67.

Rowley, J. B. (1999, May). The good mentor. *Educational Leadership, 56*(8), 20–22.

Rudney, G. L., & Lea, K. (2000, November). *Teachers' implementive and innovative approach to multicultural education.* Paper presented at the annual meeting of the National Association for Multicultural Education, Kissimmee, FL.

Shadish, W. (1998). *Some evaluation questions. Practical Assessment, Research, & Evaluation, 6*(3) [online]. Retrieved June 15, 2002, from http://ericae.net/pare/getvn.asp?v=6&n=3

Shepston, T. J. K., & Jensen, R. A. (1997, March). *Dodging bullets and BMWs: Two tales of teacher induction.* Paper presented at the annual meeting of the American Educational Research Association, Chicago, IL. (ERIC Document Reproduction Service No. ED407364)

Silberman, M. (1996). *Active learning: 101 strategies to teach any subject.* Boston: Allyn & Bacon.

Slick, S. K. (1997). Assessing versus assisting: The supervisor's roles in the complex dynamics of the student teaching triad. *Teaching and Teacher Education, 13*(7), 713–726.

Slick, S. K. (1998a). A university supervisor negotiates territory and status. *Journal of Teacher Education, 49*(4), 306–315.

Slick, S. K. (1998b). The university supervisor: A disenfranchised outsider. *Teaching and Teacher Education, 14*(8), 821–834.

Soltis, J. F. (1986). Teaching professional ethics. *Journal of Teacher Education, 37*(3), 2–4.

Sudzina, M. R., & Coolican, M. J. (1994, February). *Mentor or tormentor: The role of the cooperating teacher in student teacher success. Education and human resources: Putting the pieces together.* Paper presented at the annual meeting of the Association of Teacher Educators, Atlanta, GA.

Tellez, K. (1992). Mentors by choice, not design: Help-seeking by beginning teachers. *Journal of Teacher Education. 43*(3), 214–221.

University of Minnesota-Morris Teacher Education (2002). *The elementary education program handbook.* Retrieved June 28, 2002, from www.mrs.umn.edu/academic/education.html

Veal, M. L., & Rikard, L. (1998). Cooperating teachers' perspectives on the student teaching triad. *Journal of Teacher Education, 49*(2), 108–119.

Wasserman, S. (1999, February). Shazam! You're a teacher: Facing the illusory quest for certainty in classroom practice. *Phi Delta Kappan, 80*(6), 464, 466–68.

Weaver, D., & Stanulis, R. N. (1996). Negotiating preparation and practice: Student teaching in the middle. *Journal of Teacher Education, 47*(1), 27–36.

Wilson, E. K., & Saleh, A. (2000). The effects of an alternative model of student teaching supervision on Clinical Master Teachers. *Action in Teacher Education, 22*(2A), 84–90.

Winitzky, N. (1990, April). *Structure and process in thinking about classroom management.* Paper presented at the annual meeting of the American Educational Research Association, Boston, MA.

Winitzky, N., Stoddart, T., & O'Keefe, P. (1992). Great expectations: Emergent professional development schools. *Journal of Teacher Education, 43*(1), 3–18.

Winograd, K. (1998). Rethinking theory after practice: Education professor as elementary teacher. *Journal of Teacher Education. 49*(4), 296–305.

Wooley, S. L. (1997, February). *What student teachers tell us.* Paper presented at the Annual Meeting of the Association of Teacher Educators, Washington, D.C.

Yinger, R. J. (1999). The role of standards in teaching and teacher education. In G. A. Griffin (Ed.), *The education of teachers (98th yearbook of the National Society for the Study of Education,* pp. 85–113). Chicago: University of Chicago Press.

Yopp, H. K., & Yopp, R. H. (1996). *Literature-based reading activities* (2nd ed.). Boston: Allyn & Bacon.

Yopp, R. H., & Yopp, H. K. (1992). *Literature-based reading activities.* Boston: Allyn & Bacon.

Zeichner, K. M., & Liston, D. P. (1987). Teaching student teachers to reflect. *Harvard Educational Review, 57*(1), 23–48.

Zheng, B., & Webb, L. (2000, November). *A new model of student teacher supervision: Perceptions of supervising teachers.* Paper presented at the annual meeting of the Mid-South Educational Research Association, Bowling Green, KY.

Index